The Voyage of a Veteran

Encouragement
for the battles
of life

Russell L. Reid

ISBN 1-58169-230-7
For Worldwide Distribution
Printed in the U.S.A.

Axiom Press
P.O. Box 191540 • Mobile, AL 36619
800-367-8203

A NOTE OF CLARIFICATION:
It is here affirmed that each and every person mentioned in a negative fashion in this book is fictitious. When negative comments are made, they are for the sake of describing an actual scene or account. No intent is made to defame any person in this writing.

The name, Robert A. Sykes, is assumed to be fictitious. After extensive inquiry, such a person as mentioned could not be located. It is the author's assumption that the name was given by an imposter.

TABLE OF CONTENTS

DEDICATION

This book is dedicated to the memory of Laura Elizabeth Criner, my granddaughter. Though her life was short, she left an everlasting joy for her family and all who knew her.

ACKNOWLEDGMENTS

Where would I be without my family and friends who believe in me and who do not hesitate to tell me when I'm wrong?

This book would not have been written without the encouragement and prodding of Patricia Erwin. Thank you, Patty, for not giving up on me.

Don Harold Lawrence also aided my efforts to bring this work to completion. Part of his contribution was this: "Russell, we have got to complete this book in the twentieth century. You are not going to live forever." Thanks, Don, for advising me to add a first and last part to my manuscript.

Another personal appreciation is extended to Mrs. Judy Hendrix who typed the last two copies of the manuscript. Job didn't possess all the patience.

A heartfelt appreciation is offered to my former teacher and friend, Dr. Joe Ben Irby, who wrote a mot generous Foreword to my book.

I am deeply indebted to Mr. Keith Carroll, my professional author coach who took an interest in my work and managed the project through to completion. I also extend my thanks to Ms. Micki Milam who introduced me to Mr. Carroll.

Last, but not least, I wish to express my gratitude to my family and many other good people I have known for so many years. Whatever merit this book deserves, you have contributed immensely to its completion and publication. I am grateful to so many people for so much. It has been our voyage together that aided my longevity of life and my enjoyment of living.

FOREWORD

A teacher is proud when a former student does something noteworthy, such as writing a book, and he is honored when asked to write the foreword for that student's book.

I am that teacher, and the Reverend. Russell Reid is that student. It was my privilege to have the author as my student at the Memphis Theological Seminary. While older than most of the students (having entered college at age 35), he was a serious one. He diligently pursued his studies while serving a parish charge and fulfilling his family obligations.

Francis Bacon wrote that some books are to be only "tasted" and some are to be read only "in parts." This is not such a book. It should be read as Bacon said, "wholly"—not only for information about the author but also simply to be enjoyed.

Many of the experiences related in this book are quite humorous, while others are quite sad. The book is filled with interesting and exciting experiences. The author has the ability to laugh at himself, which is a quality of a good person.

As the title indicates, the author is a veteran of World War II. He was drafted before he finished high school. But the work is about much more than "the voyage of a veteran." The book is also about the author's experiences as a farm boy, a farmer, a good family person, a husband, a father, a minister of the gospel, and a retiree.

As a minister of the gospel, working for the United Methodist Church, the author served parishes in the city of Memphis, small towns, and rural areas of West Tennessee. In some instances, he brought healing to churches that were seriously divided.

The author has incorporated an earlier work into this one. Some of the contents of the work were hatched while he was riding a tractor on his farm.

In the midst of all of the interesting experiences recounted in this work, the faith and philosophy of life of the author are also made manifest.

Readers who know the author personally will come to know him better by reading this book. Those who do not know him personally will come to feel that they do know him after they peruse the pages of this delightful book by a true friend of humanity and a devoted servant of God.

Joe Ben Irby, Ph.D.
Professor Emeritus of Theology
The Memphis Theological Seminary
of the Cumberland Presbyterian Church

PREFACE

This book is about people I have met on my journey of life. The emphasis of the total work gives special attention to unforgettable people—persons who have had a positive effect, and some who have left negative impressions, upon the minds and spirits of some of their associates.

The story of Robert Sikes is just one illustration of a negative person causing mental perplexity for others. It wounded my self-esteem to realize that I was taken in by a con man such as he.

This book is divided into four parts. It presents, in chronological order, accounts of some of my experiences with other people. It is not my life story. My intent was to share experiences that involved issues that impact our society.

Part I is a thumbnail sketch of my early life, but it is also symbolic of the early life experiences of many other people. It speaks of some fun times, as well as some unpleasant periods. I grew up in an era when adversities were more common than were affluence and comfortable living.

Part II deals with the interaction of persons and the social, mental, and physical effects of those interactions. This section comprises episodes from my civilian and military encounters within our complex society. It reveals that a person can be influenced by the generosity or imposition of his associates in his struggle for survival.

Part III includes accounts of humor and stress played out on the stage of one's chosen profession of service and daily living. It has much to do with the "other side of the story" that may remain obscure from persons uninvolved in such experiences. This section, plus the Sikes story, was written 20 years ago. Yet, I believe its emphasis on life and living is as relevant now as it was at that time.

Part IV provides something of an overview as the author reflects upon past experiences of his lifetime. Hopefully, a backward look will help to provide a positive direction for the journey of life ahead.

These have been some of my experiences, and I am sure that many other people can say, "Yes, this has also been a walkway of life that I, too, have trod— sometimes with joy and gratitude, often with uncertainty and fear."

In regard to military veterans, I hope I have helped to provide a degree of insight into what your military experience was like.

Voyage of a Veteran is not confined to a military journey. It also embraces some implications of the totality of individual living. I stress the importance of applying Christian principles to everyday living and human associations.

My purpose in writing this book is to emphasize the relationship between faith and fortitude. I wanted to help individuals by providing examples of appropriate ways to respond in both positive and negative settings and to encourage them to make appropriate adjustments when necessary. I seek to lift the spirits of persons who may have lost faith in themselves and others as they have gone about the task of living from day to day.

Left: *Reid (left) and Marvin Stark*

Bottom: *The General Weigel docked at Oakland, California, on October 21, 1946. The author was on board at that time.*

Left: *Author's wife
Christine, "The girl
dressed in red."*

Bottom: *Author's
parents and siblings.
Seated:
Papa and Mama
Standing (left to right):
Terry, Roland, Frank,
Jessie, Pauline,
Russell, Noel, and Lyle*

Author's daughter, Jean Criner, and her family:
Left to right: Elizabeth, Jean, Ivan, Clay

Author's grandson, Clay Criner and his wife, Julie

Left: *Author's grand-daughter, Elizabeth Criner, to whose memory the book is dedicated.*

Bottom: *Russell and Christine on vacation*

PART I
WHO AM I?

Chapter One

Life on the Farm

We flip the pages of time and take our private and corporate places amid the ever-changing circumstances of life. Every person has a part in the successes and failures of humanity. There are various factors that affect our contributions to the total human story. I think a person's background has a great deal to do with where he goes in life and which routes he takes to get there. Inheritance, environment, and our will become a part of our life story.

A person cannot travel far on the road of life without realizing that not only are there adversities to overcome but also there are some people who will help him and others who will try to lead him astray. Some deeds and circumstances—whether self-created, or brought about by another person or situation—may bring pain to the mind and sorrow to the soul; however, faith, determination, and fortitude will usually erase the negative impact or, at least, make it bearable.

One of the most basic questions of man is, Who am I? According to the Bible, all humans are created in the image of God. I once read a story in which a man, who appeared to be prominent, joined a distressed and crudely dressed person who was sitting on a park bench. (To the best of my memory, it was Plato, the Greek philosopher.) The man asked the stranger on the bench, "Who are you?" The troubled soul responded in a very straightforward fashion, "I wish to God I knew."

Thinking of my family and others whom I cherish helps me to better know who I am and to appreciate them more fully. A person must discover his identity to fully understand his gifts and the areas of service for which he is best suited.

It makes me uneasy to hear a speaker close his remarks with the words, "God bless the United States of America." Such a statement is in no way like The Lord's Prayer—especially, "Thy will be done, on earth, as it is in heaven." I would rather hear, "God bless the peace-loving people of the United States and all peace-loving people throughout the world." That expression alone would influence my opinion of a political candidate and help me to know more about the speaker.

My good friend Reverend Don Lawrence has been reading my manuscript and told me, "Russell, you need, first of all, to tell the reader who you are and where you are coming from." My response to his suggestion is that I am a person who has known many unforgettable people. It is my privilege to relate some family and public matters that involved some of these unforgettable people. I hope they will be pleased with what I have written. I also wish to introduce to the readers some people who have had a positive effect on many lives.

I am a member of a large family. I believe that family, friends, and even people-at-large all help to make life what it is, and I owe a great debt of gratitude to so many people for so much. I believe that readers will say, "Yes, I know where you are coming from. That is also a part of my story."

My parents and two of my older brothers are deceased. Papa, as he instructed his children to address him, died when he was 93 years old. My mother died when she was 97 years old. My brothers Noel and Terry were both over 70 when they passed away. My two sisters, Jessie Mai (Des) and Pauline, are still living. Of the remaining brothers, five are military veterans; three of us served during periods of military combat.

Three of my brothers and I inherited some of our parents' interest in family descendants. One day in March 2004, the four of us made an all-day trip to Pocahontas, Tennessee. The distance from our central point of departure near Jackson, Tennessee, was nearly 60 miles. It was a most enjoyable outing. As far as I can recall, it was the first time since childhood that the four youngest brothers had spent an entire day together. The entire family gets together occasionally, but this was something special.

Our destination was an area near the Tennessee-Mississippi line. The object of our travel was to locate some cemeteries where some of our oldest relatives were buried many years ago. Our niece, Betty Lynn Hutchinson, had conducted some prior research, which aided our efforts. We found three burial places where the Reeds had been placed during the eighteenth century.

One may notice I have just spelled the family name differently from the name we now use. It is my understanding that my great grandfather decided to break camp, change his name, and move away. Perhaps he just simply became jealous of his brother, who will be mentioned shortly. He was responsible for our family group under the new name of Reid. Traveling a great distance must have appealed to him. He drove a wagon team of mules all the way to Texas. He was rewarded well for his efforts; he went into the oil business and became financially wealthy.

His son, my grandfather, was a teenage boy when they moved. As he and his father neared Memphis, Tennessee, the young fellow began to strongly encourage his father to buy him a new pair of boots. When his efforts failed, he angrily exited the wagon and headed out for parts unknown. Not knowing where he was going, he finally located near Ripley, Tennessee. In a few years, he was married there, and that is where my father was born.My grandfather remained there and died as a young adult. Not many years ago, I stated to my eldest brother, Noel, "It all happened for the sake of one pair of shoes. Aren't you glad he got off that wagon?" I suppose the moral of the story is "Unless you have walked in my shoes, you don't know where I've been."

Perhaps the most interesting event during the day was the discovery of the gravesite of our great-great-grandfather, a Presbyterian minister. The people of that community still give him credit for starting the Presbyterian Church in that area. But that's not all he started; he also became the father of 15 children. He contributed democratically to the cause of the Civil War with two of his sons fighting on the side of the Union, and two in the Confederate army. The marker for the wives was somewhat unusual—one stone, wide enough to accommodate the names of his spouses: Mary, Catherine, and Mollie. The husband's tombstone, bearing his name, was in line

4

with his wives' tombstone, which was about 12 feet away. That left a noticeable empty space.

That visit took place on a Tuesday. The following Monday, my daughter Jean Criner and I accompanied my wife, Christine, to the hospital in Jackson, Tennessee, to see a doctor. The waiting room was somewhat small. It was filled with people waiting for their names to be called. They were very friendly, and many began to converse freely. Christine happened to inquire of a nice, young, friendly lady, "Where do you live?" She answered, "Pickwick, Tennessee." I informed the stranger of our recent journey to her area and told her our mission had been to find the plots of our ancestors.

When asked what she thought of the unusual burial spot of my great-great grandfather, she replied, "I do not know. Maybe he intended to add to his list of wives!"

I commented, "Well, if he did, I suppose he became disappointed, because he died when he was 65, the same year his youngest son was born."

The so-called Great Depression had a negative impact on most of the nation's people in the early 1930s and lasted until the beginning of World War II. A common statement helps to clarify that era in our history: "The rich get richer, and the poor get poorer." Many people still remember that time well.

My family farmed for a living. We raised cotton for a cash crop, corn for livestock feed, and hogs for our consumption. During those years of financial adversity, cotton became very cheap. All matter pertaining to daily living demanded a conservative application of funds for food, clothing, and shelter. Even schooling for the children underwent an assortment of adjustments. This sort of adverse experience caused many people to be reluctant to venture out financially, even as the economy began to gradually improve.

This led to a common consideration by parents. They wanted their children's lives to be better than theirs were. The baby boomers of today were expected to have a more comfortable lifestyle than did their parents. The depression became a part of the people who survived it. For those who grew up during that time, it was an experience never to be forgotten.

I sometimes wonder if those trying circumstances did not leave a lasting impact on my father's approach to future financial success. The old statement, "A burnt child is afraid of fire" seems applicable at this point. Being born on a farm and being reared in a rural environment during a time of depressed economy had much to do with molding my future life.

Childhood on the Farm

The first money I ever earned was from selling rabbits. I constructed some box-like traps that worked quite well. It was always a thrill to check those devices each morning and inventory my catch from the night before. I sold the rabbits for 10 cents each. Some of the children at school wanted to know where I was getting all of that money.

At an early age, we children were taught to work in the cotton field, feed the livestock, cut wood for fuel, and milk the cows. Each child knew his assigned chore and carried it out faithfully.

One of my most unforgettable moments of farm life took place on an occasion when Papa, Terry (at this time, a teenage boy), and another man were hauling a load of loose hay. The driver crossed a mound of dirt and turned over the wagon. This covered Papa and Terry with a tall stack of loose hay. Terry was the first one to work free. He came out calling in a loud voice, "Here I am; here I am!" My father dug himself out and slowly replied, "I was not as worried about you as I was myself. I thought you would get out all right." I do not know how a boy in the old days ever became an adult.

There were no motorcycles or four-wheelers; furthermore, there were very few bicycles available for recreation. But there were animals that could be very entertaining at times.

When I was about eight years old, Terry decided he was going to teach me to be a cowboy. He placed a halter on a Jersey yearling and instructed me to climb aboard. I hesitated. I told him that I could not ride that calf—and for good reason. My legs were too short to grip the sides, and I couldn't stay on. Since my brother was five years older than I was, he was able to persuade me. He gave the instructions, "You just get on your belly with your head to the rear. Hold the calf in his flank, and he cannot throw you off."

Everyone who has ever seen a rodeo knows that a bucking strap tightened around a horse's flanks is designed to ensure action. Finally, I decided to give it a try. I mounted the calf as I had been instructed—my head to the rear with my chin resting on the end of the Jersey's protruding backbone and my hands gripping the animal's flanks. Terry stripped off the halter, and I began a short but rough ride. That calf began to buck like a bronco horse. Every time his feet hit the ground, my face made contact with his tailbone. I did not want to fall off, but I was too uncomfortable to stay on. Suddenly, I turned loose and rolled off onto the ground. I have not practiced that sport since that day.

As children, we looked forward to hog-killing time and Christmas. When the hogs were processed, we enjoyed some very tasty food. All of that ham, sausage, and bacon really went well with my mother's hot biscuits. With 10 people around the table, it took a lot of food to satisfy our strong appetites.

When processing time came, Papa would usually exchange services with our neighbor, Mr. Lewis McBride. He was a likeable fellow; he always took the time to show personal interest in the boys in our family, as well as his own sons. He would tell us funny stories of events that had happened many years earlier. When he died, we lost a very good friend and neighbor. I am sad that he didn't live long enough to see his son become the president of a bank in Fulton, Kentucky.

Christmas time was a very special occasion for my family. It was then that we received most of our new clothes. We were all so impatient for the holidays to arrive; we were anxious to see what Santa Claus would bring us.

One Christmas, Roland and I decided we would play a prank on old Santa. A part of our meat house was reserved for storage. That particular winter, Papa had stored a big bin of cottonseed in that room. My brother and I were playing in that pile of seed when we accidentally found two toy dump trucks. We later received them as part of our holiday gifts. We hauled cottonseed around in that room for several days before the trucks showed up on Christmas morning; however, the day before Christmas, we knew we had made our last secret deliveries before we had to replant them in the mound of seed. We decided that it would be neat to cause Santa to do a little extra digging in order to recover the toys, so we placed them much deeper than they had been when we discovered them. We thought it would be funny to make Old Santa scratch around in that big pile in the dark of night to get his merchandise. I really do not think we were bad boys; we just wanted to have a little holiday fun.

Roland is still "trucking" around. He is a successful businessman and still has time to do some traveling. I suppose he would say that the most traumatic event he has experienced was witnessing the death of an airplane pilot.

Before my brother went into public business, he was a farmer. He had employed a commercial crop-duster to treat some crops. The pilot, when making a low-level turn, raked a nearby tree. The plane immediately plummeted to the ground, mortally wounding the pilot. Roland pulled him from the burning wreckage and held the still-conscious man's head in his lap until he died. Roland immediately flew his own plane back to his private landing strip, which was located on the farm, landed, and never flew it again. I'm most certain that was an unforgettable experience for him.

My father was, by nature, a quiet man. We children were taught to respect his solitude. He revealed this trait in his daily interactions with other people. This characteristic was evident in his participation in church related activities. As the men of the congregation stood around under the large red-oak tree beside the church, telling events of the past, he usually remained quiet. He joined in the applause only when those who spoke more freely told a humorous story.

Our church was a large white building located near a sharp incline in the road that passed nearby. The site for the sanctuary had been donated years before by my mother's father; thus, it was a special place for her.

Church Life

While we children were young and still at home, the family filled our old Chevrolet car to full capacity and rode the six miles to attend worship services on a regular basis. One of the most unusual and interesting memories I have of those events of worship was the seating arrangement of the parishioners. Before the service began, the mothers would gather up their children and take seats on the left side of the sanctuary. (A man would not have been caught dead sitting with the women and children.) The group of men remained in place until the pianist began to play the first hymn. At that instant, the group would form a single line and enter the building—much like a graduation class moving in place to receive their diplomas from the school principal.

The male choir members peeled off and entered the choir area, and female choir members handed them hymnals that had been opened to the appropriate page. Papa did not sing, so he took his seat among the silent brethren.

Years later, the congregation purchased a new church organ, removing two pews from the amen corner to provide space for it. This created a clash among some of the church members. But Papa was not a part of the ensuing stressful situation. He again remained silent.

My father was a great sitter. He could take his seat, cross his knees, and talk to a neighbor all day long. My mother was 10 years younger than he was. In later years, she became concerned about his lack of physical exercise. One evening, she said, "Willie, let's go for a walk." Not moving from his comfortable recliner, he asked, "Where are we going, Jo?" When she answered, "We're not going anywhere . . . just walking." Papa put forth some easy reasoning, "If we are not going anywhere, there is no use to walk." He kept his seat.

Papa was a good carpenter. He had only a fifth-grade education, but he was very good at math. In his head he could solve mathematical equations that many people had to figure on paper. This was very helpful to him when constructing a building.

He showed much love to the grandchildren who were born into the family. He became their hero. And for one sensitive grandson, my mother became "Maw-Willie."

When my younger brother Roland was about 12 and I was about 14, we began to cause Papa some aggravation. The family members belonged to a Methodist church. A Baptist church was located a little more than a mile down the road in the opposite direction from the Providence Methodist Church. The community was known as Holly Grove. That was where we attended grammar school.

At that time, our home church was almost devoid of young teenagers. The Baptist church, however, had many interesting girls and boys who were near to us in age. (I think there were some boys in the congregation.) My brother and I would get dressed on Sunday mornings, slip away from home, walk the distance to the Baptist church, and enjoy our associations with friends and peers. Papa did not like that arrangement at all. He was partial to Methodists, not Baptists. (Years later when the Methodist Church became the United Methodist Church, he said, "I am not a United Methodist. I belong to the Providence Methodist Church.") Papa also had reservations about his boys "fooling around with those Baptist girls." Thus, his disapproval became a spoken one.

My mother followed pretty closely at my father's heels in matters of family participation. One can quickly conclude that any mother of eight children would have her hands full, being a homemaker and providing many so-

11

called common services for her entire family. I have heard her say many times, "I could hardly sleep until the last child came home at night."

In these later years, I have come to realize that her emotions must have run a stressful course as one-by-one her five sons left home for military service—three serving during a time of war.

Aside from her activities related to family, friends, and church, Mama did not have a great deal of time to do things other people were able to do. She liked to read and was a faithful church-school teacher. She was an officer in her local Women's Missionary Society group for as long as I can remember.

She enjoyed discussing matters pertaining to her family heritage. Her relatives accounted for a large percentage of our church membership. Her mother died when she was quite young, and her father never remarried. Mama revered her father, who served as both mother and father to her and her three sisters.

I can recall some interesting events that were related to her church life. This short account has to do with my cousin's mother, who was also a member of the ladies' group. One afternoon, Ernest Williamson, Jr., was dropped off at our home to play with Roland and me while his mother attended the regular session of her organization. After some time, we three pre-teen boys were about played out. I asked our visitor, "When is your mother coming to pick you up?" Ernest Junior replied, "She will be back soon." With that response, I further inquired, "Where is she?" This young fellow must have picked up some idle talk from others in his social circle, for he replied, "She has gone to attend the 'They-say' program."

My mother was somewhat of an opinionated person.

12

She viewed each of her family members as individuals and treated us as such. Perhaps we pleased her the most when we asked her questions about her ancestors and her home life as a child. She appreciated it when others showed an interest in those matters. She expected her children to agree with her in most family concerns, especially those involving her relatives.

Some years ago, I was invited to return to my home church, and I spoke during the homecoming celebration. I thought I had been courteous and considerate enough when reviewing traditionalism and mentioning people who had gone from our midst. I began to close my remarks by telling a story. Mama became very impatient with me, to say the least. She was not very talkative during the lunch that followed the service.

The story I told was about a middle-aged person who had become very successful. He was socially popular, and his financial status had exceeded his fondest imagination. All of his efforts seemed to pay vast dividends. His entire situation was very pleasing to him. This individual realized that he was giving much thought and time to the questions, Why have I been so successful? and, Where did I get such ability to accomplish so much in such a short period of time? He thought there must be a reason why it had happened. He decided it could be attributed to his family genes and that his ancestors must have been very unique people.

In order to come to terms with this issue, the man devised what he thought to be an informative and satisfying strategy. He researched his family tree and discovered that many of his relatives had been successful farmers, politicians, business people, etc. When he encountered evidence of a relative having an undesirable record, he recorded positive remarks instead of the truth.

Finally, he came to the case of his Uncle Josh. This historian was not about to tell Uncle Josh's story accurately. He could not bear the thought of telling people that his uncle had been electrocuted by the state. Instead, he recorded, "Uncle Josh was a man of his own means. He did his own thinking, and he often adjusted the truth to fit his own liking. My uncle held a chair in one of our state institutions, and when he died, it was a great shock."

My mother did not find any humor whatsoever in the story, and she did not fail to reveal her dissatisfaction to me. It seemed to me that she thought I had dishonored all our ancestors.

The nonverbal scolding by my mother did not last long. I knew it wouldn't. The last thing she said to me on my last visit with her was, "Russell, I am proud of you. I am pleased with what you have been doing for the past many years." I suppose that is the best compliment any child could receive from a parent at any time, but it becomes very special when those are the last words spoken to an individual.

I do not suppose she ever knew it, but Mama did set me up once for a near disastrous fall. I did behave like a whimpering child, but I experienced periods of time when it was difficult for me to make adjustments.

Courtship

Prior to my induction into the military service, Christine and I had been doing some interesting socializing. I believed—and thought she did, as well—we had reached a point where our relationship showed the potential to become permanent.

Just after I entered the service, Christine graduated from high school and moved to Memphis, Tennessee, and became employed at the Federal Supply Depot.

14

Upon joining the military, I became homesick even before leaving the induction station. After about a month at Camp Gordon, Georgia, I became acutely troubled by the separation from all of my loved ones. Then, I received a letter from home. My mother's letter read, "This girl that you know, all dressed in red and so pretty, was visiting friends in the community, and she was at church Sunday. I just wanted to tell you. I knew you would be interested to hear that."

I still remember those details very clearly. I remember wondering how my mother could do that to her homesick son. About that time, Frank Searcy, from Moultrie, Georgia, said to me, "We had better go into town tonight." I did not know that my troubled spirits were showing until he later said, "I was afraid you'd go AWOL." (Later in a life or death situation, I repaid my friend a thousandfold for his courtesy to me.)

I was not the only homesick soul who was battling with the strains of life at that time. I think many others felt as I did one Saturday night many months later in San Fernando, Philippines, when I walked out of a stage show being presented by the Ziegfield Follies. I remember thinking as I walked to the barracks, I have had about all of the reminders of a better way of life that I can take right now. It is difficult to describe the overwhelming emptiness that I experienced from being lovesick and homesick at the same time. I am thankful that I did not receive a "Dear John" letter like those I had seen so many times being passed around the barracks.

I thought wedding bells would ring as soon as I returned to the states. And they were ringing, just not for me. Christine kept me out on a limb for four months. I guess she was trying to determine whether or not my head was screwed on straight. I wonder if she's found out yet!

Both Mama and Christine have been very positive factors in my life. A good mother and a good wife are treasures and should be greatly appreciated. They had a way of teaming up on me at times, but it was for my own good, so they said. And by the way, Christine is a Methodist, not a Baptist.

Chapter Two

Expanding Horizons

I agree with the statement "For every plus in life, there is a minus," but would like to make a slight adjustment to it, "For every plus in life, there is the possibility of a minus."

My grammar school and high school left a lot to be desired. I attended grammar school in the community of Holly Grove. The school was located a little more than a mile from my home. My three younger brothers and I walked to school, regardless of the kind of weather we had. The elite group of the high school would zoom by us in the fancy school bus, while we waded through the mud, dust, and snow.

We had a good school. The teachers were experienced, thoughtful, and dedicated to their profession. Mrs. Grace Powell, her daughter, Miss Helen Powell, and Mrs. George Boyd were all helpful and considerate. My sister Jessie said to me not long ago, "Mrs. Boyd remained our family's greatest cheerleader all of these years."

Located in a farming region, county schools closed for some weeks in the fall to allow for students to help with picking cotton. My younger brother and I had to remain absent from school for longer than the allotted time. It became necessary for us to do some studying at home, but we had some good help.

Jessie was a teacher at another school, and her services to us were very helpful. Lyle summed up her assorted contributions when he was in grammar school. He said, "Des, I feel like I belong to you. When I'm home, you are here, and when I go to church, you are my church-school teacher. You are with me all of the time." Those words were very close to being the truth.

Our oldest sister was with the family over an extended period of time. Her husband, Edward Castellaw, was in the military service, serving in Europe, and they had never established a home of their own. Jessie taught in the public schools for most of her adult life. She retired many years ago. She is now in her 90s and is still going strong.

I sometimes say to people, "If she had not occasionally let me use her car for a date, I would still be a bachelor." Her 39 model, four-door Chevrolet was nice, and it surely did expedite romantic endeavors.

Jessie no longer has a husband, but she has four brothers, a sister, and a host of grandchildren. She and her husband never had children, but in a way, she has had more children than have her brothers and sisters; she has had all of us as children.

I suppose the only "touchy" point in her family matters has been that Mama seemed to have been a little jealous of Jessie's special place in family relationships. When visiting our mother during her later years of life, she would sometimes comment to us, "Well, I suppose you have already been by to see Jessie." I do not think that a little rivalry ever hurt anyone.

I enjoyed being in grammar school and my association with the other students. We played baseball and other games during the recess and lunch breaks. We did not have much sporting equipment, but that did not stop us from playing.

Attending Holly Grove became more enjoyable after the county began to provide hot lunches for students. We were no longer required to carry a cold lunch to school. A lovely elderly lady by the name of Mrs. Nowell made some of the best soup and cornbread I have ever tasted. I remember her with fondness and appreciation.

Entering high school brought about a new awakening for me. I had heard older students talk about different subjects being taught by different teachers in different rooms. I wondered how a person could ever learn where they were supposed to be and when to be there, but it was no problem at all for me.

The teacher I liked most was Mr. Ernest Dumas; he was the kind of adult I enjoyed being around. He was the agriculture teacher. It happened to be my favorite subject. It was easy for me to identify with that course because it had to do with farm life and the growing of crops.

High school, for me, was limited to one year, but it was where I met the young lady I was later to marry. The war and other matters that need no further explanation necessitated my leaving high school early. I am not fretful at this juncture in my life, yet I know that there was much I missed that would have added meaning to my experiences in life.

The interruption in my education required me to make a strong effort when it resumed. We are creatures of habit, and once habits become patterns, they are not easily broken. It does give some justification to the question, "Why do some people have to work so hard for what they get, while others wait for a free ride on the road of life?"

My brother Terry seems to have been a classic example. He was really the kind of fellow whom one needed to approach from various angles in order to pin down. No doubt, there are many people who would like to help me report on him at this point because he was the boy who wore the "coat of many colors."

At the funeral home the night before his memorial service, I startled a local friend of his by saying, "The rest of us had reason to hate him, but we loved him. He seemed to always receive favoritism from everyone." Terry could get money from Papa when no one else could get a cent. He enjoyed other small favors from friends and family.

Even the military service seemed to be designed to make Terry comfortable, but there was one exception. I was still at home on the farm when the story of his short trip to Africa surfaced. When crossing the Atlantic Ocean for an invasion of North Africa, his convoy of ships was threatened by a very dangerous storm. The soldiers were sitting on the floor of their compartments with their duffel bags placed around them for a degree of padding and protection. The situation was very tense, but one talkative companion made it worse when he called out, "O Lord, come down and be with us and do not send Your Son, Jesus, because this is not a place for a boy." The ships all landed on schedule, but Terry soon boarded another one for the return trip to the states. In the early stages of the North African campaign, the U.S. Army captured some German soldiers, and they became prisoners of war. They were being transported to the United States for incarceration. Guards were needed for the trip, and Terry was lucky enough to be chosen as one of them.

After landing on the East Coast, my brother was sent to California for military police duty. His new assignment was that of riding trains from California to destinations within the country. He and his partner slept in nice hotels, ate their meals in restaurants, and then made their way back to the West Coast. This was their mode of service until the war ended. That sort of duty caused the general military population to resent the military police. But, that was an exception to the rule. All such service was not that easy. Terry was just lucky.

PART II

Chapter Three

Doors Are Symbolic

Unforgettable people remind me of free-flowing doors. Many move in either direction. A person moves in the direction of his choices, desires, and inclinations.

I took the following story out of chronological order and moved it to this point. Doing so helped me to focus upon the cultivation factors that run deep into the mental, spiritual, and physical mannerisms of many persons. The following story of Robert Sikes provides factual embodiment to the question, Why do people sometimes do as they do?

On a Friday in April 1983, I had planned to take off from my ministerial work and leave the city. But the weather was damp, the sky was dark, and rain came down sporadically. I was in my church office working on my sermon for the coming Sunday morning when I heard a knock on my door. I quickly turned the doorknob and was confronted by a nearly hysterical man. At first sight, I was convinced that this stranger, attired in wrinkled clothing and displaying frustrated emotions, was actually a very cultured and socially refined person.

"Do you have a school here at your church?" was his first utterance to me. He continued, "I was told by someone at the church about two miles down the street that you have a children's day-care school here. Is this true?"

I replied, "No, we do not have such a school here."

Noting the anxious man's desire for further assurance, I informed him that we had only a church school that met each Sunday morning. He was visibly disappointed.

Wanting to help this person, who appeared to be in his early 40s, well-educated, and distraught, I invited him into my office. He began to speak in a low and troubled voice, verbalizing much sorrow, disappointment, and frustration. "Why," he asked, "did they tell me that? How could anyone be so cruel as to send me on this long walk here? Now I must return over the same distance and then go back those miles to the mid-city area. That will be a long walk."

As he began to take his seat, we introduced ourselves. From his manner of speech and vocabulary, I could tell he was not in the habit of being in such mental strain and financial trouble. As Dr. Robert Sikes sat nervously on the edge of the black leather office chair, he gave me another surprise. "You would think," he said, "that a person with two Ph.D. degrees would not find himself in this sort of circumstance. I have a doctorate in psychology and another in the area of sign language for the deaf."

I reminded him that, sooner or later, many people meet with unexpected adversity and that he should not be too hard on himself. I told him, "I have a small fund that I may use at my own discretion, and I will help you."

"Sir," he hastily replied, "I did not come here seeking money. I came here seeking quick and temporary employ-

ment. I cannot accept charity. I have my pride. I came to
this country when I was two years of age. My parents are
naturalized Norwegians, and all of my life, they instilled in
me that if I could not provide for my own needs, I must do
without."

As Dr. Sikes spoke, I believed he was being apologetic
for his national heritage, and I interrupted his continuous
lamenting. "Yes, but we are all foreigners. At different
times, we all came from somewhere else." However, this
man possessed a great ability for cutting in on the ragged
edges of our conversation.

"But, sir, if you would be kind enough to listen to me a
few minutes, I would like to tell you my story. Then I must
go. I have something that has to be done. I appreciate
your financial offer, but it's too late for money." His words
rang a bell in my mind. The Easter season and its historical and moral ramifications discussed in sermons and
church school brought back to me the Judas story all over
again. Judas felt compelled to leave the other people and
deny Christ. This man indicated that he was about to do
to himself what Judas did to Jesus.

"But I do need to talk to someone and explain why I
am as I am, now. This is important to me. I need to talk."

I assured Dr. Sikes that if he would tell his story, then I
would listen with much interest. Though interrupted at intervals by quick wipes of his moist eyes, his words flowed
in majestic pace.

"I have been the president of a school for deaf children
in Dallas, Texas, for 15 years," he said. "My school was
heavily funded with money provided by the Federal government. But, due to all of the cutbacks as a result of the
adverse economy, my school lost its aid and had to close.
Rather than return to my wife's parents in Phoenix,

24

Arizona, and live on them for several months, I decided to call on the various schools and colleges in West Tennessee and seek some sort of employment. My wife, daughter, and I have been living and sleeping in our car for the last several days and nights."

Gazing at my personal scholastic credentials hanging on the wall, Robert continued his remarks. "I see that you graduated from Lambuth College, Jackson, Tennessee. I had just returned from that school to Memphis when I made the decision to send my family ahead of me to Jonesboro, Arkansas, where a friend of mine teaches at the local college. My intention was to join them later after seeking emergency employment. I had completely run out of funds and did not know what to do. Then, someone told me he thought the large church on the corner of Elvis Presley and Holmes Road had a day-care school for children, and they might need the kind of service that I am prepared to render. I caught a bus to that location and then heard the disheartening news, 'No help needed.'"

"It was then," Dr. Sikes continued, "that I decided on one further strategy. I decided to approach the president of one of the local banks and seek a loan. I had not been in a position to personally need such services and was somewhat unfamiliar with the process of borrowing money but believed that with my background and proper identification, I could arrange a loan for $150."

Dr Sikes then asked me, "How do you tell a strange banker that for 15 years you have been employed as a school president and appear as I now appear? Look at my shoes. I've walked holes in them. The banker got around to the question of collateral. I had already told him of my scholastic endowments, and all I can say about that is, if you ever need to seek quick financial relief, don't tell anyone you have an education. When I informed the bank administrator that I have no property, he said to me, 'Man, you are worthless.' That's what did it."

"Did what?" I inquired. "What do you mean when you said, 'That did it'? What are you saying to me? I'm going to be very frank with you. You have said enough to involve me in your situation. Let us be open and honest with each other."

Dr. Sikes needed no further prodding. "I knew what I must do," he said, "in order for my wife and daughter, who is now 11 years of age, to be cared for. I'm worth more to my daughter dead than alive. I have a great deal of life insurance. When I leave you, I am looking for the tallest building I can find. If I am worthless, I want to take care of my family while I can."

Since I knew something had to be done soon, I confronted my visitor, using as much persuasive speech as possible. "Man, I don't have the time nor the will to polish my words so that they may match the degree of verbal perfection you now use. Sometimes, when I get in a hurry to speak, or find myself in a tight spot, I revert to my days on the farm and my hog trough philosophy. I'm going to give it to you straight. I'm not going to have your blood on my hands. You say you are hard headed in your convictions! Let me tell you about the great gifts you have to give to humanity. I tried talking to you about your family. You say you love your daughter so much, and I am sure you do. Let me tell you something. I have helped raise a daughter. I know what a child needs most of all. If you destroy yourself, thinking money is what your child wants most of all, you will be very wrong to do so. You will be of no good whatsoever to her if you are dead. That money will make her sick at her stomach. And besides, suicide is probably not covered in your policy. She needs you. If you are as committed to her welfare as you say you are, you can eat dirt until things get better."

At this point, the church secretary, Mrs. Carothers, came over from her office in another section of the church to bring me a copy of the Sunday bulletin. "I didn't know," she later told me, "who you had in your office, but it surely must have been someone who had really been bad for you to be that loud in conversation."

As our conversation continued, my visitor said to me, "But the banker, a supposedly responsible man, has convinced me that I am worthless."

I strongly argued, "You are not worthless. I've never seen you before, but I see a person who is terribly upset and temporarily distressed, yet who is of great value to so many people. I believe every word you are telling me," I continued, "but, just for the record, will you allow me to see your personal identification?" He quickly provided a picture i.d. I then responded, "I knew it, but I just wanted to see it for sure."

I continued to encourage Robert Sikes to be reasonable. "Friend, put some of your learned skills together. You know what's wrong. I can't tell you one thing you don't know, but you are frustrated. You have temporarily lost control of yourself. You are trying to escape, and you have chosen the shortest—but worst—possible route out."

My attempts to get him to focus his attention upon himself, his wife, his daughter, or anything else produced little noticeable results. That was when I knew he was determined to commit suicide.

I thought it would be difficult for me to handle it if the five o'clock news reported this man's death. That was the cue for my last move. I believed I was still holding one trump card, but it had to be played carefully. I was assured that this would be my last opportunity to save this person from himself.

"You have said that you have an 11 year old daughter and that she desperately needs food, clothing, and shelter. I've already told you what your death will do to her. Think about the fact that she will be compelled to grow up without a father. You speak as if you are the only person who has ever once considered such a way out when becoming acutely troubled! She will be compelled to go through life knowing that her father wasn't strong enough to survive a hard time in his life—that you deserted her when she actually began to need you the most."

Robert's eyes expressed a kind of friendliness that had not been present until that moment. My internal emotions were raging. I didn't really know how upset I was until the matter was over. I actually experienced a terrible sense of fear, but I knew that progress had been made. The mental vision of a fatherless child seemed to shock this troubled soul back to his senses and me back to mine.

"Robert, I'm going to give you $150, which you so desperately need. You said it would take that much to get with your family and to go on to your wife's parents in Arizona. Here is the phone. It will not cost you one cent to call her and inform her that you are coming to Arkansas to get together again. This money will be yours with no strings attached."

"No, I can't call them," he said. For an instant my emotions took another dive as I began feeling I had failed. "They will be on the Jonesboro campus somewhere, but I don't know where. My friend, the teacher at the college, is the only one who will know where my family is, and he is in class at this hour. But I could be there before I could get in touch with him. There is a man at the medical center here in Memphis who has agreed to help me get there once I return from this visit."

This was the first and only time I was suspicious that his story possessed a tinge of falsehood. The idea of calling seemed to create a degree of uneasiness for my visitor. And too, if he had desired to remain at my church and render a short-term service, why did he have someone standing by to ensure his travel on to Arkansas? But I soon dismissed this thought, and we continued the troublesome dialogue.

Suddenly, Robert offered a proposition, "I will take the money under one condition."

"Any condition," I interrupted, "is progress. I have never in my life had such a hard time giving money to any person. This is a new experience for me. If you were an addict or an alcoholic, I would not give you one cent. However, I can tell that is not your problem."

"But these things, I do not do," he quickly responded. "I smoke, and if smoking in your office offends you, I'm sorry. But I am not a liar. Yes, I smoke, and I'm not trying to hide it."

Trying to soothe his mental aggravation, I said, "That's what the ashtray is doing on my desk. Enjoy your cigarette. It'll make you feel better."

"Sir, you can't give me one cent," my guest continued. "But I will borrow the money at 13.9 percent interest for six months. That is the going rate. Fill out a note, and I will sign it and repay the money in September of this year. You may depend on that."

"Is $150 enough?" I asked. "I am prepared to beat that a bit if you want me to."

"No," he said, "that will get us where we need to go."

I began to compose a statement note—more for his satisfaction than mine. I began, "I, Robert Sikes—" when he suddenly interrupted me. My intended borrower did have his pride and suddenly caused me to laugh softly and politely.

"Make the statement to read, 'I, Dr. Robert A. Sikes, owe Bethany Parkway United Methodist Church the sum of $150 plus 13.9 percent interest for six months, which I promise to pay in full on the date of this note's maturity.'"

Robert signed this hastily formulated document with a very handsome style of writing. I started to tell him we would just knock off the nine-tenths portion of the interest, but I was afraid that would kill the whole deal.

We then got into my pickup truck, which I prized very much, and started to leave for the downtown area. My companion also liked my truck. He called it the Texas Cadillac. As we pulled away from the church, Robert made an interesting discovery.

"I think I know why I was sent to your church," he said. "I noticed that you have a nice playground for your children. I'm now sure why someone was mistaken about a school for children."

On the way to the bank to cash the check, I informed Dr. Sikes that I would be pleased to purchase a new pair of shoes for him. My offer was rejected with an explanation. "These shoes will do me until I get to Arizona," he said. "There is something I haven't told you until now. I have employment, beginning in September, at Baylor University in Dallas, Texas, with a salary of $40,000 per year, as professor of psychology."

I implored him to allow me to buy some comfortable shoes for him. I would enjoy knowing that, come September, he would be strolling over the Baylor campus in my shoes. We all have a degree of pride, do we not? We should.

As our journey continued, we talked about several things of interest to me. This was my opportunity to listen and be briefed. Robert spoke of how one man owned a vast section of the city of Dallas. But most interesting were a few brief lessons in the sign language for the deaf. As we neared our destination, I sought once again to avoid any reoccurring idea that might interfere with Dr. Sikes' intention of rejoining his family. I said to him, "Robert, you are all right now. I can determine that, but please allow me to have one further word with you." This he did willingly. "You spoke of the people who closed your school as 'deserters of deaf children and people having no heart.' If you go now and remove yourself from being able to someday help children again, you are going to join that same crowd about which you just spoke."

With a beautiful expression of relief, my fellow traveler said, "Sir, I'm not. I promise you." He continued, "I want to say something. I hope you will not be offended but will understand the manner in which I speak. I love you."

His smile and my grin met in mutual admiration, and I said to him, "Oh, how I wish I could hear those words more often." We enjoyed a comfortable laugh, and my new friend prepared to depart.

I paused in front of the drug store at the Baptist Hospital. We shook hands and said good-bye. Smiling, Robert hastened inside to catch his ride to Arkansas. As he crossed the street, I actually felt as if a part of me were going with him. In a sense, I felt as if a door were closing between us, and I wasn't ready for it to close. I hoped that I would meet again with him some day and have another conversation.

Because the last two hours had left me so weary, I was unable to relax once I returned home. I listened very closely to the five o'clock news that evening. The day was damp and humid—conditions that professionals in the human sciences believe contribute to human suicides; however, I just knew that Dr. Robert A. Sikes, professor of psychology, Baylor University, Dallas, Texas, would not be a part of that newscast. He wasn't, but I am still waiting for his letter assuring me that he made the trip just fine. My door of concern is still open. I just hope and pray that he doesn't close it.

Chapter Four

Pride: An Enemy to Personal Stability

The word "pride" is both a positive and negative descriptive. In this writing, the word is usually intended to have a negative connotation. The particular emphasis on a subject will explain its intended usage.

Many of the unforgettable people I have known were endowed with philosophies of life that had been nurtured by both positive and negative modes of personal conduct. A common statement says, "We are what we eat." We are also what we hold to be useful, interesting, and rewarding.

The Bible is very specific in its stance on the negative attributes of an individual or group of people. "Pride goeth before destruction and a haute spirit before a fall" (Proverbs 16:18).

As I see it, pride lends itself to the insistence upon personal separateness of an individual. It thrives upon a demonstration of personal superiority and minimizes the uniqueness of others. Pride persuades many individuals that they are free to join or to separate themselves from others as they so choose. In a social setting, this may be appropriate, but no one should ever ignore the welfare of others. The Holy Bible gives us many examples of this

33

truth: "And the Lord said unto Cain, Where is Abel thy brother? And He said, What has thou done? The voice of my brother's blood crieth unto me from the ground" (Genesis 4:9-10).

Personal success in daily living depends upon a continuous dialogue between an individual and those who are in his immediate surroundings. I was reminded of this fact in one of my psychology courses in college. During a class discussion, I asked my instructor, "Does a psychologist ever find himself in need of consulting another person in the same profession?" His response was a negative one. His face paled a bit, and his eyes seemed to quickly focus on a nearby book. I suddenly realized I had asked this mild-mannered and courteous professor an embarrassing question. After a short and silent pause, he responded in a quiet voice, "Yes, we do."

The doorway to slow human betterment has not been opened by a lack of wisdom and poor understanding but by the mistaken and casual idea that private and corporate efforts count for very little. Such an attitude is easily encouraged by one who offers pretentious concern for another's welfare, while offering no evidence of genuine compassion. Perhaps this is best described as deceptive friendship. The prophet Isaiah was a stern rejecter of hypocritical expressions of concern and comradeship. "The people honor me with their lips, but their heart is far from me, in vain do they worship me, teaching as doctrines the precepts of man" (Isaiah 29:13).

Christians, as well as non-Christians, often appeal to the negative dimensions of progress. Why does one seek to take the wrong approach to life's endeavors? There are one or two possible alternatives. A person may hold a negative view of Christian theology, or he may take the course of least resistance. Exposing one's weaknesses requires a form of courage, but magnifying weaknesses is a senseless act of self-depravity. In her recent book, Virginia R. Mollenkott makes an interesting point:

> Don't misunderstand me. I had achieved a Ph.D., and on the surface I looked anything but indecisive. My lack of balance stemmed from a tacitly assumed concept of God which had turned me into a drifter. One day a friend put his hands on my shoulder and shook me. "If you don't like your circumstances, do something about them! You are not a victim!"[1]

Wounded pride combined with a sense of rejection may encourage aggravated conflict, resulting in a state of hopelessness. Thus, unity of cause and effort ceases to prevail over frustration and a sense of failure. I believe that Dr. Sikes felt as if he was considered a second-class citizen of a first-class country. Perhaps he confused parental hardships with national allegiance and freedom. Although the nation was not his problem, the circumstance of his family's survival in a new country resulted in a rigid lifestyle for each member of his family. The gifts of many years had created a cushion. When financial aid was terminated, not only did scholarship suffer but also positive pride for the institution suffered. A generous government is held in high esteem, but when it loses much of its reputation for gracefulness, it is held in low esteem. Generosity is seldom a one-way street. Donations are usually made with an unspecified intention that, someday, the investment will pay appropriate dividends. If a recipient does not understand that condition, then his pride may be subjected to intense pain.

Recently, a friend said to me, "For every plus in life, there is a minus." I understood this to mean that for every gift, there is a cost borne by someone, and the receiver should be prepared to respond in a positive fashion when compensation is demanded.

After World War II, the military went to great lengths to persuade veterans to re-enlist. The main pitch was directed toward the veterans' nostalgia for "lost feeling of security."[2] The military forces had made vast investments in the training of military personnel, and with the Korean War looming, in order to increase combat forces, recruiting services were appealing to the discouragement and lost pride that was being experienced by many recently discharged soldiers. I strongly considered such a plight for myself.

I related to the predicament of young men who wanted to get a start in civilian life but who lacked advantages such as a proper education, financial aid, or business experience. This situation was true for many men and women who had returned from the war, married, and attempted to establish a home and find an acceptable occupation. In my community, there were very few houses that were suitable for rent, almost nothing available for purchase, and few lots available for the construction of new houses. Business and agriculture were so locked in by the non-veterans that it created a difficult social and financial climate for veterans.

If Dr. Sikes thought he had received ill treatment, he should have been around during the last years of the 1940s. His frustration was expected to be of short duration. Many of us who were born in America had little hope of gaining relief from semipoverty for many years to come. That not only tries the souls of men but can also completely destroy their sense of positive pride. I was compelled to work for 15 years before considering the possibility of formal education. Yet I became convinced that if I retained a vigorous desire to share in community progress, then it would be impossible for the private elements of society to close the door of opportunity in my face. I agree with Pascal, who said, "There is a God-shaped emptiness in all of humanity, and only God can fill that emptiness." I also believe personal effort and responding to the best that one knows to do provide the raw materials out of which individual character and success are molded.

As long as a person has hope, that person can usually find a way to work out his adversities and retain a sense of personal integrity. That is a privilege that our national constitution does not deny to anyone. Both native-born and foreign-born individuals can take comfort in that assurance.

License of privilege and favoritism are not the same. It is impossible to interpret the events of history from within the framework of man's humanity to man. To participate in human events is part of the journey of faith. Faith in external factions has not been the dominant factor of individual and group expression throughout the centuries of human struggle for survival. "Violence between persons and groups is the dirty but open secret of history."[3]

The Bible gives us an ongoing description of human struggle within the context of humanity. "For his anger endureth but a moment; in his favor is life: weeping may endure for a night, but joy cometh in the morning" (Psalm 30:5). Perhaps the best advice one may give to another is to say, "Hold on until things get better."

Pride produces a low profile in community participation and in religious expression. It forces the Christian out of his/her role as a suffering servant and into viewing Christianity as little more than the embodiment of the redeemed. Such a view ignores the emphasis of evangelism and the teaching of Jesus about the contributions to human life that all persons are expected to make.

Empowerment by the Spirit not only moves us out to confront the world but also binds us together so that the confrontation will be the single voice of our Lord and Savior, Jesus Christ. The single voice of love speaks for the common good of all.[4]

Humility and pride make strange bedfellows. Humility is a virtue of outstanding proportions, but pride is an obstacle to the spirit-filled life. It is a negative substitute for faith and personal disciplines of morality. Human betterment is derived not only from knowledge but also by the practice of known skills. Pride is a tease and a hindrance to the process of mental comfort and spiritual maturation. It seeks to invalidate the principles that virtue is stronger than infidelity and that experience takes priority over mere belief. It is a negative postulate, offering aggravated posture to religious effort as it provides the basic means through which one comes to terms with his better self.

The practice of Christianity is not limited to the affirmation of specific codes, beliefs, and conduct; however, it should be deployed through religious institutions and personal involvement. There need to be stronger efforts made by local churches for the integration of education into worshipful experiences and expression of faith. Great minds and great faith do not have to oppose one another; they can cooperate and enhance the welfare of the believer. When these two become divided or altered by circumstance, the result may lead to mental depression and self-destruction.

In its truest sense, salvation does not address human compartments, but it seeks to redeem the whole person. The church has often been guilty of addressing the needs of individual spirits and leaving the mind and will to flounder in a limbo of anxiety. It is disturbing to me when I hear expounders of the faith become critical of the good earth, which God intended to be mankind's Garden of Eden. It is depressing for me to hear a call and challenge to blindly follow anyone or any movement or to hear the promotion of a dichotomy of mental, moral, and spiritual awareness.

Faith is both operative and influential. The Christian faith, as employed by institutional religion, has a definite responsibility to teach and inspire people who are not members of a particular parish or congregation. Segregation of human welfare is not in accord with New Testament theology and mission. In the Cumberland Seminarian, Dr. Clinton Buck quotes C. Ellis Nelson, who gives an interesting statement on the origin and purpose of faith. "Faith is communicated by a community of believers and that the meaning of faith is developed by its members out of their history, by their interaction with each other, and in relation to the events that take place in their lives."[5]

When people lose respect for Christian principles, their trust for the institution or larger order of Christian authority is depreciated and restricted. The result is one of excessive dependence upon the self to satisfy needs. With each degree of success, pride in oneself becomes stronger unless such personal arrogance is intelligently challenged. When a person struggles with pride, not only are personal values questioned but also the state of self-hood receives a damaging blow.

Because she had been compelled to play a minor role in the affairs of her family, a loss of will had become the plight of Mrs. Sikes. Adding adversity to isolation can quickly result in a sense of insecurity for the troubled victim. Virginia R. Mollenkott offers this comment regarding a meaningful existence:

> Many a time I had discussed with sophomore literature classes a poem by T. S. Eliot about hollow men who are also stuffed men—hollow of meaning, that is, but stuffed with the straw of trivia. These men have "quiet and meaningless" voices, "paralyzed force," and shifty eyes. Because they cannot bring their ideas to reality, their impulses to action ...until finally their words end, "not with a bang but a whimper."[6]

Confusion is the testimony of the troubled, the response of the timid, and the result of yielding to a negative external force. Sikes' wife may have been a strong person, but the suppression of her personal role may well have restricted her participation in the drama of her lost husband. I am not in position to judge or to evaluate the relationship of Dr. and Mrs. Robert A. Sikes. However, I can speculate based on my observation of him during our two-hour conversation. It is certainly unfair to assume anything negative based on one traumatic meeting. I am convinced that the most critical issues arose for consideration and discussion. His relationship with his spouse may have been so secure that there was not reason for considering this matter with a stranger; however, reasonable evidence suggests otherwise.

My visitor referred to his wife only once during the entire time we were together. He was very specific when discussing insurance money for the welfare of his young daughter, but no one else received such consideration. I came to believe that he had only minor concern for his wife.

I will not attempt to draw any conclusions about the nature of the relationship of this man and his wife, but I will seek to focus upon related matters so that the reader may answer some questions for himself. I did not have all of the facts needed to thoroughly consider this case, and even if I had, I did not consider myself qualified to offer a complete solution to such a complex issue. Yet, I found myself asking some assorted questions: "Why does Mrs. Sikes play such a minor role in this tragedy?" "Why does her husband depend so strongly upon introverted efforts in order to solve their corporate problems?"

There are times when appropriate questions are more in order than are unsure answers. Perhaps his wife's understanding and love were taken for granted. Did she share equally in the administration of family concerns? Was she expected to abide by her husband's decisions, with no questions asked?

There is noticeable conflict evident in the relationship of some individuals, brought about by the so-called educated person versus the uneducated individual. This disparity is very stressful to many marriages. This attitude of diversity may foster conditions of jealousy, a sense of personal supremacy, and estrangement between two otherwise happy and well-adjusted persons. Recognition given to a partner who holds one or more professional degrees may result in an attitude of competitiveness in the spouse if the spouse is not as well educated or receives less professional recognition.

If Mrs. Sikes found herself competing with her husband's desired image among his intellectual peers, she may have felt lost. Her husband had developed such a need for personal security that he may have become blinded to his greatest sustaining source.

Already having two strikes against him, Robert Sikes was about to strike out. The reason was clear, and the outcome was certain. A widow and a fatherless child were to be the result of his inability to finish his ballgame of life. He was running from field to field and was leaving the best players stranded on base.

If this man was indeed the professional scholar he professed to be—and that I thought he was—he may well read this summation of his case. He sought to regulate the format of our discussion and to determine its end result, but perhaps he would be surprised to discover that during the time he was building his sad story for my personal response, I was gaining insight into his personality and moral character.

When a person is out of sorts with himself, he sees very little that is good in anyone. When people have faith in themselves, they have faith in other people and other sources of sustenance and are able to move their focus away from themselves and onto other areas of experience that validate their personal composure. The faithless person not only invites weakness but also restricts the contributions of the faithful. It is difficult to helplessly stand by and watch someone perish. But when one is forced to play a minor role in a family tragedy, there is little else he can do.

In my opinion, religion had played a minor role in the affairs of my visitor. He lamented the fact that, immediately prior to our discussions, someone had said to him, "Oh, just trust God and things will be all right."

My reply was, "Surely, I believe the Lord will help us, but saints have problems too. Help comes as we seek to help ourselves." With this, my troubled friend readily agreed. Yet, I still held the opinion that the Christian faith was of secondary importance to him. Dr. Martin E. Marty hinted of the tragedy when he wrote, "participation on humanist soil … Yet it is invisibility of religion, not infidelity, that prevents many scholars from accurately assessing power in the world today."[7]

Successful participation of partners in a social and financial order not only helps to create a dimension of security but also leads to the harmonization of other family concerns. I recall hearing an author say during a radio interview, "Happiness is not the ultimate goal in a life. The developing of the ability to respond in a positive fashion is the most important issue in the life of any person."

It is important for individuals in a relationship to sit down together and evaluate their interests and philosophies of life in the light of their own personalities, abilities, and expectations for themselves. People may be restricting their lives' attainments because they expect too little of themselves. But at the same time, they need to be reasonable in their demands upon themselves and others. Every person must live and work within the framework of personal ability and the willingness to give expression to one's own individuality, but always doing so with the realization that one's greatest dreams and expectations may never reach fulfillment.

I have a profound belief that a wife does not need to make the constant announcement that she is inferior to her husband or strive to prove she is equal to, or better than him. Persons do not have to remain imprisoned by believing that to excel in a unique and recognizable fashion, they must measure up to every person.

Chapter Five

Retreating From Competitive Living

I had my unforgettable conversation with the man who posed as Dr. Robert A. Sikes more than 20 years ago, and I have not heard from him since. That September I mailed a letter to the location in Phoenix, Arizona, which he had given as his temporary address. This was also supposed to have been the address of his wife's parents. However, the letter was returned and marked "unknown." I wanted to know about this man's personal welfare. I also wanted to remind him that his promissory note was past due.

I had begun to wonder if I had not been the victim of a cleverly conceived plan of deception. Some information accidentally given to me recently by a friend reinforced that suspicion.

The United Methodist ministers of both Memphis districts met for an all-day program of study and discussion. At one point, one of the ministers in the meeting described his encounter with a distressed man who held two Ph.D. degrees. This stranger, seeking employment, had come to him in the spring. The circumstances he described paralleled my experience so closely that I later questioned this minister for more details regarding his visitor. We agreed that we had encountered the same person. The only difference between the two stories told to us was that Dr. and Mrs. Sikes were separated in the later version. I am now compelled to realize that my confidence in this man was not justified.

The surfacing of these more recent events caused me to wonder if my visitor was a con man, if he committed suicide, or if he was ashamed to be confronted with his unpleasant past. When a person loses the will to succeed, he is tempted to withdraw from the social and moral arenas of competition. And he would forfeit his integrity and disregard his personal responsibility rather than have to put forth the effort required for him to succeed.

I think there must be rational answers to this man's irrational behavior. Because of my continued interest in this case, I later applied a renewed effort to discover the truth. I received the following reply from a professor at Baylor University: "The name, Robert A. Sikes, does not appear on the register of professors and instructors at this institution but will continue to seek information on him from this source."

The expression of social integrity in human interaction is a virtue of great importance. One such philosophy of life may well be that I, like you, am on a pilgrimage. I cannot tell or show you very well how to travel on your journey, but in my best self, time, and circumstance, maybe I can help you to see yourself in a better light and to have a greater appreciation for yourself. Maybe I can help you see that you possess virtues you never knew you had. Maybe I can be a good neighbor to you and encourage you to remain an active, positive competitor in society.

The present generation includes many people who have sought to place a major emphasis on limiting social and moral values. Many seek to excuse their poor participation in a respectful society by appealing to the injustices that they claim to have inherited. That the so-called older generation is not living up to its professed moral integrity is an argument made by many who are well pleased with this poor record. Such awareness seems to help excuse the imperfections of many members of the younger generation. Recent evidence points to the fact that 1984 marked the first time in history when high school seniors were less skilled than their parents. There are reasons for this, and they do not lie in the area of lost opportunities.

I never cease to be amazed and startled by the constant negative reports from relatives and friends who are in the teaching profession. They complain of the disinterest and restrictive attitudes of so many of their students. So much time and effort is wasted on imposing discipline in the classroom that the process of teaching and learning is sorely restricted. This is one noticeable consequence when individuals and groups refuse to participate in proper community activity and insist on self-reliance for their social and mental advancement.

School Experiences

Graduating from college at the age of 39 remains one of the high points of my life. In my early adult life, I was compelled to endure strict and demanding military discipline. Even though I knew it was designed to aid personal survival in combat, it never gave me the sense of accomplishment that I derived from my scholastic endeavors. I suppose I am what some might call a "late bloomer," but over the years I have wondered if frost did not hit that bud before it reached full maturity!

For me, school was not only a mental exercise but also

a social achievement. Many of my best friendships were developed while in a classroom with students half my age. I think that experience has caused me to better appreciate people of all ages. One friend asked, "Mr. Reid, what are you doing here in school, preparing to die?"

My answer was, "Yes."

Perhaps this explains my willingness to accept a school assignment even though I felt unqualified for the task. The principal of a nearby high school requested that one of the students in my social theories class compose a syllabus for a course in economics. When my professor called for volunteers, there were none. He then approached me with the assignment. My reasoning was, "Mr. Exum, you know I haven't had one single course in the study of economics. I do not feel qualified for the project."

My instructor replied, "Russell, I am mindful that economics is not your area of study, but that is not the question I asked you. I asked if you would be willing to prepare the requested syllabus." Seeking to please my professor, for whom I had the greatest respect and appreciation, I agreed to do the assignment.

I formulated my personal strategy and began my study of high school economics. I had an intense desire to contribute in a personal way to the program of institutional learning for other young people. But my greatest motivation was to show the teacher, who had faith in me, that I was trustworthy. My system of composition worked quite well. I made a B on the project, which was considered to be a term paper. My syllabus was acceptable to the high school officials.

The desire for personal participation is a positive endeavor. Its virtue lies in the seriousness of effort to obtain satisfactory results. Its destination is reached when response aids the wholeness of human character and mortal awareness. Its rewards are never confined to a state reached. It results in an attitude such as that mentioned in Philippians 4:8, "Whatsoever things are true, whatsoever things are honest, whatsoever things are pure, whatsoever things are lovely, whatsoever things are of good report; if there be any virtue and if there be any praise, think on these things." Within this biblical context lie many individual and corporate regulations and privileges; one is that persons have the right to be different from one another. But even such freedom must be disciplined by certain restrictions.

Truth Brings Freedom

Centuries ago, Jesus stood on trial before Pilate. He was asked, "What is truth?" Truth for Jesus at that time would have been freedom from false accusations and detainment. Surely, in this time of civil unrest and trials, he gave renewed thought to the validity of the verse, "Ye shall know the truth, and the truth shall make you free" [need reference]. Had it not been for sin or the unjustified freedom of others, Jesus would not have been treated as he was during the closing days of his life on earth.

Freedom to be oneself is limited to a conditional freedom. A person has the right to be herself, but not to the point of imposing upon the legitimate rights of others. I have become very familiar with many of the tricks some elderly people impose on other people. It is certainly true that a decline in mental, social, and physical activities will limit mental alertness. But I do not agree that as a person ages, his mind is what deteriorates first. Advanced age is often used to take advantage of persons who are sensitive to the welfare of family members and friends.

49

Many elderly people reach a point where they feel secure about expressing negative feelings that have lain dormant for many years. Some actually resent the death of their spouse and react in an ill and troublesome fashion toward those who are doing all they can to make them comfortable and happy. I remember quite well one lady who complained that her husband would be a semi-invalid for many years and that she would be compelled to nurse him and spend much of their financial savings in order to keep him alive. This was not what happened. When her companion of many years died suddenly, fear and guilt added to her sorrow, causing her to become resentful of other kind people and neighbors.

I believe that the mind is more akin to the heart than it is to other physical members of the body. A few years ago, Mrs. Mary Pilcher, a member of my ministerial charge, told me that she and her husband were on their way to church when they passed a neighbor's home and were inspired to stop. The father and his young son were sitting on a pile of firewood near the house. His wife, who was the mother of the child, had recently died, leaving both husband and son in a state of depression and insecurity.

Mrs. Pilcher inquired of the father if they would like to go to church with them that Sunday morning. His reply was, "No, it will take us too long to get dressed for church. We will not bother you today."

But the neighbor insisted. "I will bathe and dress your son. It will not take too long." Her help was reluctantly accepted, and these two grief-stricken people quickly joined others in an hour of public worship.

A few days later, the child's father called upon the Pilchers with a most unusual story. "When you and your wife stopped Sunday morning to invite my son and me to attend church with you, I had already decided to take my little boy's life and then kill myself. I was so torn up over the death of my wife, and my heart was so full of sorrow that my mind was out of control. If you had not come when you did, we would have been dead in a few minutes."

Withdrawing from other people may take many forms and result in numerous ill consequences. We do not live in a perfect society, and unless a person evaluates humanity on the basis of some positive characteristics, as well as negative experiences encountered, she will soon develop the opinion that "man at his best state is altogether vanity" (Psalm 39:5).

While on a short study program last summer, a friend and I were robbed while we were asleep. Some 300 ministers attending two annual conferences were on the Middle Tennessee College campus. I thought that was one of the safest places in the world to spend a few days of work and worship, but my idea about that was changed.

This incident caused me to recall a similar event. Paul Sutton was a 19-year-old military trainee in our company at Camp Gordon, Georgia, during the closing months of World War II. Only a few of the men there were near enough to their homes to visit them for a few hours at a time during our basic training. But Paul often left on a weekend pass and returned with delicious homemade cookies and other foods unfamiliar to military mess halls. During this time, two men, who were much older than him, became very attentive to this young man, and he responded by sharing his treats with them.

On the surface, this appeared to be friendship, but this relationship came to a sudden end about two days before we were to leave for a short furlough that was to be followed by an overseas assignment. Paul had saved some money to spend while at home on the ten-day visit. No one other than his two new friends knew of his financial planning or his secret hiding place for his funds. He discovered that his money was gone. He later confided in some of us that he had no doubts about who the guilty parties were, but proof could not be established.

It was no small concern for our fellow soldier that he had been robbed, but his most intense sorrow was the awareness that the men whom he had befriended had treated him so unkindly. The other people in our barracks pooled our contributions so that Paul's trip home would not be delayed. Although this event happened more than 38 years ago, it is still very clear in my memory. I can image that Paul Sutton has also remembered this cruel act for all of these years—not so much because he lost his savings, but because a door of friendship was closed by two thieves whom he had completely trusted with his secrets. Such a betrayal may have caused Paul to be a little suspicious in all of his human relationships since that time. Such a loss of faith in humankind can be a tragic thing.

Dr. Sikes had allowed what he considered to be one major rejection or personal imposition to regulate his evaluation of people as a whole. As we talked, I developed the opinions that he did not entirely trust me and that he resented the church as a benevolent entity. He was quite hasty in reminding me that the institutional church sought to hide itself behind closed doors of pretending to care for distressed people. I did not impose an argument or debate at this point. I did, however, remind my stressful guest that if the Church were to be evaluated on the basis of what it does not do, instead of on the record of what it has accomplished, then its credentials as an agent of mercy and reconciliation would not be too impressive.

A person does not lose a cause unless that person becomes a victim to it. Although the effort may never lead to fame or fortune, the energetic exercise of one's convictions keeps the individual motivated and determined. A positive principle forced to live in a dormant environment is much better than a silent surrender to the status quo. I am reminded of the words of Beverly Madison Currin as she quoted from *The Fellowship of the Ring*, page 110.

> The road goes ever on and on.
> Down from the door where it began,
> Now far ahead the road has gone,
> And I must follow, if I can.
> Pursuing it with weary feet.
> Until it joins some larger way,
> Where many paths and errands meet.
> And whiter then, I cannot say.

The value of endurance should never be minimized. Patience and persistence are responsible for the success of many undefeated persons. Such determination on the part of one of my long-ago neighbors temporarily aided his efforts of courtship. There was no electricity in our rural community in those days, and kerosene was used as fuel for the lamps. Sarah Jones resided with her sister and her sister's husband. Tom Craddock, considered by some to be somewhat slow-witted, persisted in his efforts to date Sarah, but with little cooperation on her part. Seeking to discourage her suitor from calling without prior notification—without offending him—Sarah notified her would-be-friend that her brother-in-law was complaining about their sitting up so late at night and burning his coal oil. Tom also did some fast thinking. The next time he called unannounced, he just happened to bring along a container of fuel.

I do not think Tom ever reached the place where he could appreciate the true meaning of Matthew 25:2, which says, "Well done, thou good and faithful servant: thou hast been faithful over a few things, I will make thee ruler over many things." But his commitment to the cause of courtship and his restless desire to be in the company of Sarah earned for him several more occasions of visitation.

Chapter Six

Caught in the Crossfire

Society is cradled in a competitive dialogue between individual intelligence and the impact of slow public acceptance of change and solutions for problems. This condition can dilute individual effort and frustrate personal progress and welfare.

Personal discipline is necessary in order for one to survive the pitfalls of such an unpredictable society. Individual stability is the product of constant and prolonged allegiance to norms of proven value. A person's conduct may be virtuous or immoral, but discipline helps one to excel or endure. The type of discipline decides the quality and character of the end results.

I entered the military service in early March 1945. At the time, I had never been more than 100 miles from home. I had not been subjected to society at large. Man's inhumanity to man was quickly thrust upon my awareness and my conscience. This is why so many of my reflections are of war and are sanctions of peace as well.

The will to survive is the most basic feature of the human nature. Every thoughtful person has some degree of fear of failing. In writing this book, I have some concern that I may be rejected by a large number of people.

In the next several pages, I will be saying a great deal about the military service and some of my experiences as a member of that vast assemblage of human beings. When I mention the fact that I was a military policeman, some current soldiers and military veterans may decide they have read enough. As a general rule, MPs (or "Maw's Pets") were highly resented by the rest of the service personnel.

The following accounts do not paint a pretty picture, but I hope my comrades will hear me out before they cut me off. For some of us, World War II did not end on September 2, 1945. The six months that followed involved a daily business of saving lives, for me, as well as others. That did not make a hero out of me. I did not volunteer for such duty. I was drafted. The war ended while I was crossing the Pacific Ocean, and when I arrived in the Philippine Islands, I was assigned to the 814th Military Police Company. I had been trained as an infantry assault troop member. My first combat duty was to have been as part of a sacrificial force landing on the coast of Japan. Based on past experience and military intelligence, 90 percent of this invasion group would have become war casualties had the invasion taken place.

The atomic bomb changed all of that, but my adjusted duty was no "piece of cake." And I do not apologize to anyone for the service rendered in my alternate duties.

I write this in the first person, but my fellow soldiers were doing basically the same things as I was. I can recall many incidents when the lives of soldiers were on the line, and we went to their rescue, often at great danger to ourselves.

On one occasion, I personally saved a fine fellow's life. James Price came to our company from a paratrooper

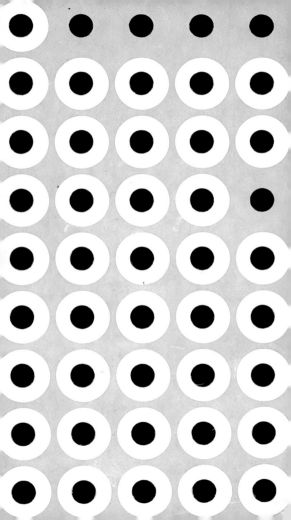

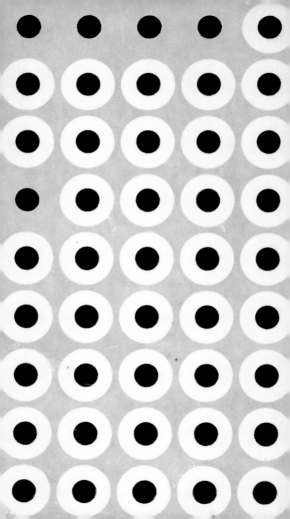

unit. Jumping was certainly in his blood. Price jumped off a stranded Japanese oil tanker, immediately took the cramps, and could not swim around the beached vessel to safety. I managed to rescue him.

On another occasion, my good friend made his move to kill a young second lieutenant. I am not going to comment on whether or not the officer deserved such a reward, because I, too, was party to the harsh and unjustified treatment. I quickly said to Frank, "If you kill the man, they will shoot you."

He related to me, "No man is going to do this to me and live to tell about it." Two lives were spared because I was able to prevent the disaster.

As the fighting on the battlefields ended, the soldiers who had been killing the enemy on a daily basis found it hard to adjust to peace the next day. So, many would drink anything that resembled alcohol. On numerous occasions, I participated with my associates in dragging the poisoned and intoxicated men from the streets and highways and preventing them from being crushed by the constant flow of military traffic. At that time, to safely cross the highway, a person had to run. These men were not criminals. They were battle-fatigued soldiers. Some 100 members of our company saved as many as possible from self-destruction.

It was a sad and sobering experience to witness the destruction of people who had survived the battles with the Japanese only to be destroyed in such a needless fashion. In all of my 80 years of living, with the exception of being the father of a very great daughter, I deem my participation in that part of my military service to be the greatest contribution I ever made to the cause of humanity.

The MPs were regular visitors to the hospital. Rescued,

crazed, violent, and dangerous parties had to be carried to the emergency rooms for treatment. And so did many who would have died from the results of drinking that poisonous "black label" alcohol the natives had concocted so that they could steal the soldiers' money. The escort trip to the hospital was no enjoyable experience. The patients were placed on sturdy beds or tables. Two policemen would remove their gun belts, straddle the person being treated, and try to hold him in a prone position while the medics pumped out his stomach. That was something like riding a bucking bronco. Male nurses normally attended to that sort of emergency patient, but one night, a lady nurse came in to lend a hand. One ungrateful fellow announced his hostility for the military police in a forceful fashion. To paraphrase his words, he accused us of being "hen-house-attendants." That was when the lady nurse informed us, "This is where I came in," and turned and walked out of the room.

After a few weeks of this sort of thing, the aggravation eased quite dramatically. The combat soldiers were hastily being deployed to the states, and the military began to ship in American-made drinks.

A major problem that remained for the police was the sailors. Since our base was located on the waterfront, ships came and went on a regular basis. Every time a ship docked in the nearby harbor, one could depend upon some new experiences. Those sailors always wanted to fight, and fight they did. It mattered not to them that the MPs carried loaded 45 pistols on their hips. When the men became intoxicated, they did not know who anyone was and did not really care. And too, we could not go around shooting people who became violent. During my period of service on that base, I knew of only one soldier who was killed by a military policeman. But I knew of many incidents where people were seriously wounded.

I do not want to be guilty of reciting the police log for one day, but two or three further descriptions of activity may help to explain why I said our work was very hard and demanding. I said earlier that this was not going to be a pretty picture.

Driving through San Fernando early one night, I happened to look into a vacant area to the side of the street, and I noticed one sailor simply slaughtering another. I abruptly stopped the jeep and walked up to the place of battle. I had never seen a young man who had been so severely beaten, and he was still receiving blows. My partner was off to the side and came on the scene a little later. I called for the two to stop fighting. "There is no use for you boys to beat up on each other," I shouted. They did stop. The wounded fellow managed to move away, but the "beater" walked up and stood close to me. I thought he wanted to talk. But suddenly his fist flew past the end of my nose. If that blow had landed, he would have put me to sleep. In order to prevent a knockout punch from landing, I quickly grabbed the man around the body, but he threw me to the ground as if he had bounced a ball.

After some time on the ground, I began to equalize the misery and finally managed to subdue the individual. My partner came on the scene. We picked up the addled attacker and placed him in the rear of the jeep. He came back to reality and kicked Marvin Stark just below the nose with a hard black-heeled oxford slipper. Then the situation took another turn. Stark's mouth popped like the breaking of a heavy stick. Stating his murderous intentions, he dropped his leg-end of the load and in a flash drew his weapon. I then dropped my end of the luggage, grabbed Stark, and had a hard time keeping him from pulling the trigger.

My involvement in that scene can perhaps best be described by saying that the clothes I was wearing had to be replaced by new ones. They were not only soiled, but they were also ripped and torn.

Before moving on to a different subject, I will mention one other narrow escape. Before Stark became my service partner, I had another partner for one day. Mascullar was handsome, smart, and well-built. Whenever we asserted (apprehended) a sailor, we simply locked him up for a few hours for his protection, and then we released him. Usually, no charges were filed. On one occasion, we arrested an unruly guy, and while we were transporting him to the police station for safekeeping, he landed a blow to the right side of my head. I scrambled to pull myself back into the driver's seat. I hung onto the steering wheel and locked the lower part of my legs against the panel board of the vehicle, up-righted myself, and avoided wrecking.

I stopped, looked over at my dignified partner, and became about as angry toward him as I had toward the man who had hit me. There he sat, never changing his position—just looking at me without saying a word. He was supposed to keep an eye on our unwilling passenger, but he had viewed the scenery instead. I suppose Mascullar thought he had come along for decoration. He was all "spit and polish." He sat there in the front passenger seat with a forward look as though he had a ringside seat at a beauty review. However, that day ended his career as a military policeman.

When pondering the past of long ago, I realize that life did have some interesting moments, even in a war zone. One day, late in the afternoon, a call came into the police station. The distressed speaker was calling from a Merchant Marine ship that had recently docked in the nearby harbor. He requested that the police come to his ship and arrest a man. His advice was, "You will need plenty of help, because this is a very mean man."

The sergeant in charge assembled six of us, whom he called his most seasoned troops, and we headed for the waterfront. We did not know what to expect, but, prepared for combat, we boarded the vessel. The word had been going around among the military personnel that "those tin-can sailors are tough." Because of the frantic call of the skipper, I wondered what sort of mayhem awaited us.

Someone led us to a room where our prisoner was waiting. There sat a man who was about 40, dressed in a nice blue business suit. He was so neatly dressed that an observer might have thought he was expecting to attend a wedding or a funeral. (Merchant Marine seamen were allowed to dress in civilian clothes when not on duty.) The sergeant in charge said, "Sir, let's go." He promptly rose to his feet and walked along with us. I remember thinking, This is a little embarrassing. Six of us, fully armed, walking along with a man who appeared to be a model citizen of our country.

En route, someone asked this man what had happened. His answer was, "We docked last night and began to have a little party. Some of the fellows had a little too much to drink, including the captain, and a fistfight broke out. All that I did was to beat the ship's captain. That's why he thinks I'm such a mean man. But I'm really not. He had it coming." (I bet that statement will make some sailors smile!)

When we arrived at the police station, we decided that our guest did not need to be locked up. All of the soldiers in our company were in their early 20s. We had commissioned officers who were much older, but they did administrative work at our company headquarters.

We hastily conferred among ourselves and concluded that locking this man up would have been much like confining one's own father in a jail cell. We decided to set up a bed for this nice, friendly man in a vacant room of the station and to let him have the freedom to move around the place at will. We even brought him trays of food from our own mess hall. When he left, we hated to see him go. He reminded us of the folks back home.

This happened on a Friday evening. On the following Sunday morning, after our newfound friend had been our guest for two days, the captain of the ship came to pick up his estranged crew member. When he saw what freedom he had enjoyed, he became very upset with us. But he soon realized that he was on our ship, not his.

One of the most interesting persons with whom our police company was associated was a man named Addis. He was not a member of the armed forces; he was employed by the Army as a professional crime investigator. Addis was about 40 years old. One of his unique talents was that of a hypnotist. He sometimes used this to his advantage when obtaining information from a person being questioned.

The first time I saw this talented person was on the nearby seacoast. Several people were swimming and riding the incoming waves. There on the beach, a group had gathered to watch Addis hypnotize a nurse. It was very interesting.

Later, while in our company area, he had an audience of our people in the area between the barracks. Different persons were volunteering to be placed under his magic.

At that time, my duty partner was a likable fellow from Philadelphia, Pennsylvania, named Louis Petril. He was a little shorter in stature than some other individuals, with a dark complexion and a handsome body-build. While Petril was hypnotized, he really got the works. He had a nice visit home to see his beautiful girlfriend.

Addis began, "Petril, you are now going home, by plane, for a most enjoyable visit." (I understood that the show went a little beyond the legal limit, but this was our party, and no one was going to complain.) The stationary traveler moved like a puppet on a string. He carefully walked up the steps of the plane, moved inside, and took a seat. As Addis grinned from ear to ear, he continued, "Petril, lie back, relax, and enjoy your long trip across the ocean." When the plane landed in the young soldier's home city, he anxiously walked down the ramp into the waiting arms of his lovely girlfriend. All of that hugging and kissing that followed there in thin air was a sight to behold!

I later thought about the fact that Addis could have gone into a profitable business right then and there. By that time, I felt certain that all who were present would have been interested in such an enjoyable trip.

While Petril was under that hypnotic spell, someone said, "He's not asleep. He's just acting in order to put on a show." At that point, Addis slapped Petril sharply across the face; however, the subject did not flinch. I am quite sure that if he had not been hypnotized, a ferocious battle would have broken out between those two people.

Addis returned to the states aboard the same ship taken by many others from our group. One afternoon, he had an audience on the port side of the vessel. It was quite a party. Addis turned to me, as I stood by and enjoyed the events at hand, and said, "Reid, I never have put you under. Why don't you be next?" My response was, "I believe I'll pass." As I looked at those rolling ocean waves, I reasoned to myself, What if I was asleep, and this ship suddenly began to sink? Why, I couldn't even swim in that state of mind and body.

My friends began to kid me in a good-natured fashion. "Why don't you go along with the rest of us?" Well, I agreed to be the next subject, but I decided I was going to resist Addis with all of my might. The magician got right in front of me—almost in my face—and began making his spiel. I was "holding my own" until I began to notice his flickering eyes. I felt my body go limp and quickly jerked myself back under my own control. This made Addis angry. He kicked my chair and walked away. I knew I was a party-pooper, but I remembered the extent to which he caused Petril to perform in the company area between the barracks. I have never been much of a showman.

I hasten to add that all of our associations with Addis were not that enjoyable. As a professional policeman, he led various patrols into some dangerous areas of activity.

In the Philippines, rural mountainous wilderness areas are called barrios. Barrio Seviere was located a short distance east of San Fernando. It was notorious for sheltering the worst kind of criminals among the civilians. After being drafted into the police company, one of our first briefings was, "Two of you do not dare go into that place alone. If you do, you will never come out." The second warning was, "There are people here who will kill you in the wink of an eye and think nothing about it. Every day you go on duty; you take your life in your own hands." That was a real eye-opener for a group of young people who had no experience in the turmoil of humanity. A few nights before this first briefing, someone threw a live hand grenade through an open window of a small dance hall. Three MPs had just entered that building. Military personnel will know what happened. It was a slaughter.

I made only one trip into the area, with a large detachment of our men, but we were unable to make any arrests. Others went at different times but usually had the same results. Our officers believed the natives always tipped off the criminals when we approached.

I am aware of one exception to the rule about not going in as a small party. One day, one of our officers said to me, "Reid, tonight you are going to accompany Addis into Barrio Seviere." That is all that he said; no information about the assignment was given to me. Addis did not tell me who it was that we were expecting to apprehend. That was a very uneasy day for me, and the night was even worse. My thoughts were, *Why me, Lord? With all of these other people in the company—some with much more experience in this sort of thing than I have—why me?*

Addis led, and I followed very closely on his heels. I am sure the authorities had information that a particular wanted-man would be in a certain small house, and that was our specific destination. We cautiously made our way to one particular dwelling. It had a small front porch, and we silently paused there for an instant. We heard, coming from inside the house, what sounded like the click of a pistol being made ready for firing. I do not think I have ever seen a man move as fast as my leader did. In a flash, he burst through the weak door and went inside. I was very close in pursuit. I was depending on Addis for my survival. No one was present except the civilians who occupied the dwelling. We immediately retraced our way off that dangerous hill and returned to our barracks. The magician had again performed his magic, and we both lived to enjoy the party aboard the General Weigel.

Barrio Seviere has provided me with another lingering memory. When returning from that steep incline on my previous trip with the larger group, walking a little distance from the others, I thought, *Man, life surely is cheap in this place!* Why don't you sometime later speak of the cheapness of life? As I recall, I have never mentioned that incident to anyone. But that internal invitation dogged my heels for 15 years—until I entered school as a ministerial student. I don't know if my thoughts were the result of my being afraid or my being glad to be alive. Really, I think it was both.

Training people for combat involves more than physical discipline. The mind and will must undergo a transformation. In the early weeks of preparation, the training made me nauseated. I did not want to kill any human being. However, some time later, I experienced a change of attitude, *If I have to kill someone, I will.* Near the completion of my 17 weeks of training, my attitude became, *Just show him to me, and I'll get him!*

Evidently, a detachment of 5,000 troops deployed to New Guinea the first year of the war in the Pacific was not very prepared. When they first confronted the Japanese troops in battle, they killed their own officers and stamped off in the opposite direction.

This noncombat group was rounded up, court-martialed, and sentenced to five years in prison. Given time off for good behavior, they finished their sentences in about four years and were sent to Japan as part of the occupation force, by way of the Philippines. The troop ship docked at San Fernando late one evening, and this horde of undisciplined people came ashore for a night in that small town. And, wild it was!

Vast numbers of quartermasters and other noncombat forces were still stationed at our base, known as Base M. After the infantry moved out of the area, they gave the military police a lot of trouble, but they were finally brought under control.

When the New Guinea detachment came into the city, some of the locals advised them they would have to "play it cool." They said, "The MPs here are plenty rough. They are in control." The visitors responded by saying, "We'll show them who is in control. We'll take over this place tonight."

That began a long night of assorted activity. The fellows working the city area really had their hands full. The next morning, the large jail cell provided "standing-room-only." Yet, some of the customers were not able to stand very well. When I came to work early the next morning, I looked inside the lock-up and saw people lying all over one another.

Because my partner and I were assigned to a more rural area of highway patrol duty that night, we missed that segment of confusion and misery. However, we did catch one tense aspect of what must have been a group from the same horde of night-prowlers and troublemakers.

One thing that made our work so dangerous was that the entire Army base was stretched out along the sea-coast. People were sometimes destroyed and dumped into the ocean, and that was it!

Petril and I had left the city area and had come to a crossroads not far from the city. It was night, but the moon was shining, and there was only semidarkness. When I stopped the jeep, prior to crossing the intersection, some 30 to 40 maniacal people wearing military uniforms noticed the MP marking on our vehicle and made a mad rush for the two of us. If they had not been stopped, Petril and I would have become two more statistics.

We usually carried only 45 caliber pistols, but expecting an unusual night of service, Petril had gone into the supply room and checked out a Thompson submachine gun. When the group made their move on us, we were practically surrounded, so I ordered my partner to stop them. Petril jumped from his sitting position to the ground with such force that the ammunition clip, which he had failed to lock in place, dislodged and hit the ground at his feet. I thought we had reached the end of our trail, but my partner picked up the clip and rammed it, with unthinkable speed, back into the weapon. By that time, our oppressors were nearly within grabbing distance. But, confronted with that automatic gun, they decided they did not want to die. These people were not soldiers for the cause of peace; they were criminals walking around in military uniforms.

We cleared the intersection of the road and went on our way. The next day, the Japan-bound ship pulled anchor, and our lives and work got back to a normal pace. I suppose the moral of this story is that those people could not face the Japanese soldiers in combat, but they could have pulled two military policemen apart limb-by-limb. I am thankful that I did not have Mascullar for a partner that night!

Like my fellow soldiers, I was simply seeking to survive in a crude and hostile environment. We did not seek that sort of duty. We were assigned to it. There were many times when we needed our Maw's presence in order to survive, but no sensible person would have wanted to be a part of what we were involved in.

A final statement on that subject is, "The truth is the truth." Many war veterans lived to return to their homes in the United States because of the sacrificial services of the 814th Military Police Company personnel at Base M., Philippine Islands. We were Maw's Pets all right, but we were too far from home to receive any of her petting.

It was nothing short of a miracle that one day most of my company walked up the gangplank of the General M. Weigel and began our journey home. We embarked at Manila. In order to clear the island harbor, the ship had to sail north and pass the entire length of northern Luzon, before turning east toward San Francisco, California. As the General Weigel went north, it passed within clear sight of our former base at San Fernando. I could clearly see the base prison, where I had spent my last six months of service on the island. I well remember gazing at that familiar sight and uttering a short prayer, "Lord, if it need be, let this thing sink, but don't let it turn around and go back. I have had enough." That prayer might have been questionable, but it seemed very sincere at that time.

I have often considered the difference in the behavioral patterns displayed by both American and Japanese soldiers who had been condemned to death for crimes committed against other people. I have no intention of implying that American soldiers were inferior to any nation's military personnel. The record speaks for itself.

After being assigned to prison duty, we held no American prisoner who was going to be executed. However, just before my tenure began at that institution, one man, who had been sentenced to hang for the crime of rape, escaped. He was never heard from again. The man whom I replaced as prison assistant manager told me a very nerve-wracking story. He explained how the condemned Americans would sometimes go berserk, cry, and scream for relief. Some were even seen standing on their heads in the corner of their solitary confinement cells. This was also a trying ordeal for the people who were in charge of the prison at that time.

As will be explained later, I personally held some condemned enemy soldiers while they awaited execution. But the Japanese soldiers were so disciplined that they accepted their close confinement in unusual fashion.

Such descriptions of mental agony betray easy discussion, and I am reluctant to write this firsthand account of long-ago tragedies, but I trust there is a lesson worthy of learning from these distressing stories.

One episode concerns the disposition of a Japanese sergeant. He revealed no emotion whatsoever and pretended to be unable to speak or understand the English language. While his execution order was being reviewed by a higher military court, he spent his entire 30 days of imprisonment in complete silence. There was one exception. One of his guards insulted him by calling him by the name of his Emperor. He burst forth with words that were very understandable. He indicated that he felt it was disgraceful for a common soldier to be classified with his Emperor. At least, that was what he appeared to be saying.

During the time of the Japanese occupation of the Philippines (from the late spring of 1942 until the fall of 1944), captured American and Filipino soldiers and civilians were tortured, starved, and killed by the thousands. I have in my personal possession many newspaper accounts of such atrocities.

One Japanese official was so cruel and inhumane to the local civilians that an all-out effort was made by Filipino scouts to capture and destroy him. The photo of this evil person was quite deceiving—a pose of him holding his child. The mission was accomplished in a most revengeful fashion. He was apprehended one night on a back street in Manila. He was immediately killed, carried out of the city, cut into small pieces, and fed to the dogs. I have documented proof of this inhumanity to man, which, to me, defies human imagination and description. I believe that the people who were involved in that episode of human misery wanted to be sure there would not be a reincarnation of this individual.

This third case cannot be described in such short fashion. There were other POWs held in our military compound during occasions of verdicts appeals, but none stand out in my memory as does the case of a handsome Japanese lieutenant. His appearance was more like that of an American than it was like that of a person of Japanese descent. He stood about six feet tall and possessed a very refined body structure. His complexion was of a light color, and his countenance was the essence of mental brilliance.

I first became acquainted with this convicted war criminal on the day he was brought to our institution, which was located at San Fernando. He was delivered there in a straitjacket and was escorted by heavy guard. My position at the military prison was that of overall security. I was not in the immediate area when the party arrived, and the soldiers waited until I returned to the compound.

This was the first time that a commissioned officer

headed the delivery detail. I shall never forget the eye firmness of Captain Joe G. Riley from Ridgely, Tennessee, as he looked me in the eye and gave me some friendly but firm advice. "This is a very serious case, and if this prisoner should escape, my punishment would be rather severe." I later discussed the matter with my superior, Captain Frank J. Bauer, and he reassured me of the seriousness of this case. I was aware that military law provided that if a capitol offender escaped, then those responsible for monitoring him would receive the escapee's sentence. I had no desire to make a contribution to the grim business of Lieutenant Charles Rexroad, who happened to be a swinging-door specialist.

I can still visualize the kind but firm expression on Captain Riley's face as he said, "Sergeant, I have ridden 90 miles, and I have waited here to see you personally and to tell you one thing. If this one should go, you had better go with him."

I responded, "Thank you, Sir. I understand." This ended our short but very important discussion. The officer joined his party, and they began their return trip to Manila. As this detail drove away, I paused to watch the soldiers leave and thought, There goes a man who cares about the welfare of other people. Little did I know that, for approximately 40 years, Captain Riley's civilian home and mine were so near to each other. What a rich experience it would have been for me to have traveled those 30 miles and discussed the events of that day in further detail. But, this failure was particularly compensated a few months ago when I visited his son, Judge Joe G. Riley. He graciously accepted a visit from someone who had come to meet his father under very adverse circumstances.

As a safety precaution, the lieutenant was housed in a completely dark room for an extended period of time, as a safety precaution. This building was located inside a well-fenced compartment of the prison and was heavily guarded. When I informed Captain Bauer that I had chosen the security measures for the prisoner, he advised me that the Geneva Convention, which dealt with the treatment of prisoners of war, had established rules against keeping prisoners in constant darkness. Prisoners had to be exposed to sunlight on a regular basis so that their eyes would not become damaged. The task of bringing him out of his darkened confinement into the sunlight each day was done very carefully, and that was the limit of his release from the daily darkness.

During the time of the enemy occupation of the islands, this man had been in charge of the forces securing the city of San Fernando and its immediate surroundings. I thought it to be something of fate or coincidence that he should be brought back to the scene of his crimes to spend the last 30 days of his life. This lieutenant's crimes consisted of masterminding the murdering of pregnant women and their unborn babies.

Strange are the facts of long-ago events that sometimes rise to haunt us. They can speak to the sensitivity of our emotions. I expressed this point of view to a friend some time ago after a certain story surfaced pertaining to one particular man's long-kept, dark secret. He died, and the mystery behind the reason that he reserved one room in his spacious house for himself was solved. All during his adult life, he allowed no one to enter his private domain. After his death, the door was opened. The room was literally filled with obscene pictures and artifacts of immorality. My comment on this subject was, "There are no sins that lie hidden forever. Sooner or later, the past will rise up to speak to us."

This sort of mental recreation of events took place some years ago when I met a man at a Wal-Mart store in Blytheville, Arkansas. Mr. and Mrs. Cheshier, from Halls, Tennessee, and my wife, Christine, and I had gone to Blytheville to enjoy a delicious meal at a restaurant that we had patronized several times before. When we arrived, it was too early for the evening meal, so our wives did what many others do—they examined the goods of a Wal-Mart store. James and I decided to linger outside and admire a vast garden of potted plants and flowers that were located near the front entrance. That scene was a most attractive array of nature's beauty. The garden caretaker came up to us, and we began a conversation that lasted for some time. I do not remember the man's name, but I will call him John Walker. We took comfortable seats on a bench and continued to exchange information about where we were from, our occupations, and other items that were of interest to each of us.

After some time, I said to Mr. Walker, "Excuse me, Sir, but I have been admiring your fine physical posture and what seems to be perfect health."

John, in a very smooth and courteous fashion, informed James and me that he had had a good life. His occupation had involved farming and raising purebred cattle. He said, "When I retired, I took this position here at the store because I just love growing plants and flowers. Besides, it's a good hobby for me. As for my health, I am in good physical condition for a man of 68 years of age. The only real illness that I have ever had came in the form of a fever while I was in the military service stationed in the Philippine Islands during World War II."

That statement really caught my attention. I also took the same illness when I was there, immediately following the war. I inquired as to where on the islands he had been during military service. John replied, "You know, it was a strange thing. I was in all of the major combat invasions and campaigns, all the way from New Guinea to Layette on the southern end of the country, and then on to northern Luzon, to the San Fernando area. It was only then that I developed that dangerous dengue fever."

I later said to James Cheshier, "He was ringing my mental bell every time he spoke of the geographical area and its ramifications." John was about five years older than I was and had been in that part of the world long before I arrived, but I, too, was exposed to much of the lingering police work that was necessary to make the area secure after the Japanese surrender. For six months, this duty was hard, dangerous, and demanding. It was after this time of being assigned to military prison duty that I became more familiar with the aftermath of the rigors of war and its effect on the combat soldiers and the civilian population. We exchanged enough facts to discredit any idea that the stories were being fabricated. Then, his demeanor abruptly changed. John's lean, slightly wrinkled, pleasant, sun-tanned face took on a noticeable seriousness.

"You know," said John, "there was a man there in the San Fernando area during the Japanese occupation, the likes of which the world has never known! There was this Japanese lieutenant who did things that the people of the world would never believe. In addition to the atrocities committed against captured American soldiers, he and his henchmen made a habit of using their bayonets to murder pregnant mothers and their unborn children. He was captured during the fighting on northern Luzon, and I'm sure that the criminal was tried by a military court. I feel most certain what the verdict was, but I've lived all of these years since my military discharge just wanting to know for sure what the outcome was. I'd like to know just what happened to him. I could rest more freely if I just knew for certain!" John's facial expression seemed to extend far out beyond our present proximity. James and I sat in silence for an instant until this man's wandering mind had finished its review of an internal struggle.

Deliberately and carefully choosing my words, I responded, "Mr. Walker, we have both just shared enough specific facts about this subject to let each other know that we are telling the truth about that long-ago infamous Japanese lieutenant. You have never seen me before this hour; neither have I seen you before. But, I am here today to tell you exactly what happened to him." John almost jerked his body and attention in my direction. "The War Crimes Tribunal," I continued, "tried and convicted him. His sentence was death by hanging. I personally kept him under my safety and control for the last 30 days of his life, and then our department of the service came and got him. He was hanged on the gallows, which were constructed in a large gray building on the outskirts of Manila. You do not have to wonder any longer."

For a fleeting moment, relief appeared in the facial expression of my intense listener. A small but satisfied grin appeared in the right corner of John's mouth, as if to say, "The no-good piece of humanity finally got what he deserved."

There was a short, silent pause among the three of us. Then, this life-seasoned, ex-military soldier changed his expression. Although I could not read his mind, I felt certain that I knew what memories he was recalling as he remarked, "What a shame that people should ever reach the place where they would do this sort of thing to each other!" At that very instant, this conversation was terminated. Not another word was spoken on the subject. As we parted from our host, he seemed to be saying to himself, "The haunting question of my lifetime has just been answered."

I thought it quite strange that such an event should take place in the midst of the beauty of this garden and its growing plants and flowers. The doors of life sometimes open up to let in the hurt and harm of negatively disciplined people, but they also often swing wide open to let in therapy and the reconciliation of an individual with himself and with others as well.

I have shared this story with only a few people, perhaps because I wondered if anyone would believe it. I can tell a true story, but I am not capable of spinning fiction. Without exception, almost all persons with whom I have shared this incident have commented that it was no accident that John Walker and I met at that Wal-Mart store in Blytheville, Arkansas. I am inclined to also believe that our meeting was motivated by a source beyond ourselves—that God, in fact, moved to eliminate this good man's internal struggle.

For me, these are accounts of unusual and extreme occurrences. At what point does one cross over the line of lost sensitivity and conscience? Where does the restoration of a person's life begin?

Both civil and religious histories have revealed that a person does not arrange for needed strength and positive motivation by considering others to be insignificant. Although human life possesses a competitive and conservative nature, it should never reach the point of the survival of the fittest.

Chapter Seven

Doorways Should Become Pathways To Progress

All trails are not easy to travel; however, the best ones are worthy of persistent effort. Humanity cannot afford to retreat or depart from such. Doorways become pathways. I have read the fact that above the triple-doors of a cathedral in Milan, Italy, are three inscriptions. A beautiful wreath of roses is carved above one of the doors, and underneath it is written, "All that which pleases is but for a moment." Over another door are a sculptured cross and the words, "All that which troubles is but for a moment." Over the third, and central, entrance, are these words of sobering truth: "That only is important which is eternal."

Individuals exercise strong efforts to express that which they consider interesting and rewarding. Values differ, and memories focus on varied knowledge and experience, but that which we cherish, we call important and seek to protect and preserve.

I find it rather interesting that my brother, Terry, when building a rustic lodge-house on his lakefront property, purchased an old, large, heavy door that was originally a part of a now-demolished train depot. I am sure his purpose for doing this was more for sentimental reasons than beauty. It is not difficult to realize that this piece of antique building marks a definite era in American history. It is easy for me to imagine the historical date of such a time and place in our past generation.

During the Civil War, the area of Savannah, Tennessee, that was near the Tennessee River was one of much interest and was often traveled through by both boat and train. Local people, foreign people, distinguished travelers, as well as those traveling for fun and festivities, passed through this door on their way to points throughout the world. During the Civil War, General Grant lived for some time in a nearby mansion. Surely, he and many of his soldiers were frequent passengers on the trains that moved in and out of this public station.

This was long before the day of Kilroy, but, once again, something discarded by the government became an item of interest and use to a private citizen. Surely, this is one more reminder that "One man's trash may become another man's treasure."

Human history cannot be easily divided and disassembled. We are part and parcel of so much that lies silent except for our recorded past and current will to add new meaning to old experiences. Memory provides some needful substance out of which new endeavors are brought to fruition and fulfillment. The doorways we open today lead to the pathways we will travel tomorrow.

Humanity's sense of survival goes back to the origin and nature of God's creation of humanity. We are not self-sustaining organisms. Human beings were born without their permission, and they die without their approval. Somewhere in between these two truths, persons must come to terms with their specialized identities. But, cooperation between individuals and groups will be the wheels of progress upon which the current society will ride on its journey to a more comfortable and commendable way of life—not only for ourselves but also for people who will live in the future.

> *In the beginning God created the heavens and the earth. And the earth was without form and void; and darkness was upon the face of the deep. And the Spirit of God moved upon the face of the waters. And God said, Let us make man in our image, after our likeness; And let them have dominion over the fish of the sea, and over the fowl of the air, and over the cattle, and over all the earth, and over every creeping thing that creepeth upon the earth* (Genesis 1:1-2, 26).

I am mindful that this explanation of human beginnings does not satisfy the critical inquiry of many, but rational thought concludes there must have been an unusual creation for such a complex being as man to have come into existence. The fact that a human being is a living, breathing, thinking, caring person sets each individual apart for unusual attention, experience, and involvement in her own world of human activity and relationship.

Part of the uniqueness of humans is their will to survive.

> If a man would overcome obstacles, he must first of all have some supreme object for which to overcome them. His success will be in proportion to his desire to obtain that which he desires.[8]

But desires for success must find expression within the framework of a person's purpose and creation. The Christian faith affirms that human beings were created for fellowship with God. This demands orderly and applicable conduct on the part of every individual. Thus, we are admonished and challenged by our very natures to fit well into our individual and corporate places as actors or participants in human society. This demands much effort and practice on behalf of every person who would make a difference in the social order.

Perhaps the love story of Joseph and Mary, the parents of Jesus, has no equal in all of history or literature. It climaxes with awe, wonder, and beauty, but the elements of stress, fear, and self-giving characterize its nature from the very beginning. The story is made more beautiful because these two people dared to be courageous during a time of uncertainty and negative public opinion.

With the institution of the New Testament, virgin virtue took on a new emphasis and importance. I am confident that both Joseph and Mary had difficulty reconciling with the reality of the Spirit becoming flesh. Until the time of Christ, life had been especially difficult for most women. During the Old Testament period, women and mothers were commonly considered persons of restricted religious and social status. Their greatest security lay in their individual ability to complement their husband and to bear his children. Apart from this need, they were viewed as being of lesser value than men.

There is no reason to believe that this noble couple had been quick to take on the quality and character of the new social and religious order, but the reality of Mary's being a virgin mother placed a burden upon their impending marriage.

In any era or social system, for a man to unexpectedly learn that his sweetheart or future wife is pregnant creates a shock of mind and spirit that is hard to reconcile. The Hebrew word "virgin" means "a young woman of marriageable age," but Joseph gave it an interpretation of a much broader perspective. He held firmly to the newer theory that virtue in an unmarried woman meant that she had never been sexually intimate with another person.

It is not difficult to understand why Mary went in haste to visit Elizabeth, the aged mother of John the Baptist. This was not the sort of thing that was easily discussed with members of the opposite sex, especially if one was unmarried. Mary needed the support that only an understanding and sympathetic person could give.

One can but wonder about the attitude of Joseph when the community gossip that his lovely bride-to-be had found favor with another person reached him. "Why does everyone know this except me?" I am not aware of any detailed encounter where Joseph broached this matter with Mary. But common sense tells us that such conversations and inquiries took place.

During the first three months of her pregnancy, Mary abided in the home of Elizabeth because public opinion had closed the door of her return to the home of her parents. It is easy to assume that during this time Mary cried out in a state of near shock, "But, Joseph, I love you. You cannot do this to us. I, too, am confused about this whole matter. I even asked the angel who brought this disturbing announcement to me, 'How shall this be, seeing I know no man?'" (Luke 1:34). "Joseph, does our love not count for anything? I just wish I knew. . . . But there is one thing I do know, I'm sure my mind knows that my heart loves you dearly."

As far as I am concerned, this is the greatest love story ever told. It is a story where both actors faithfully and completely placed themselves into their individual roles. The plot was not rehearsed or intentionally dramatized but comes forth in a natural form because the story is emphasized more than is the performance of those involved. Just imagine the relief that came to Mary after Joseph had worked through his most pressing anxiety and developed an attitude that was based on more than public opinion and societal expediency. Possibly, Joseph spoke in much the way as did Ben Johnson in *Lights From Many Lamps,* edited by Lillian Eichler Watson:

To struggle when hope is vanished!
To live when life's salt is gone!
To dwell in a dream that vanished—
To endure, and go calmly on.9[9]

Joseph and Mary were pioneers in a new social and religious order. In order to stabilize their relationship, Joseph appealed to a divine interpretation of God. "Mary, God told me in a dream that everything would be all right. That all was going according to his plans. And, instead of sorrow and embarrassment, there would be pride and praise bestowed upon our union—that our devotion to each other would result in the expression of a sacred loyalty to the yet to be born Jesus."

These prospective parents were no longer free to act just for themselves, because the rights of others had to be carefully considered. Perhaps the older Bible story of Ruth and Naomi aided their cause and supplied a comforting thought for their consideration. "And Ruth said, 'Entreat me not to leave thee, or to return from following after thee: for whither thou goest, I will go: and where thou lodgest, I will lodge: Thy people shall be my people, and thy God my God'" (Ruth 1:16).

Joseph became a good expectant father, but only after his informative dream did he reach the place where he was willing to become a stepfather. It is not enough to say this was all the will of God and that everything fell into proper perspective. Human beings were involved, and every time such is the case, there is need for careful dialogue. Only after Joseph had met the intervention of God in a personal way, did life take on a new dimension, meaning, and purpose for the new father-to-be. Only after his love story had fully matured, could Joseph truly say, "Glory to God in the highest," and submit fully to God's will.

It is the ability to love that makes every person special and every gift unique. It was God who told the story of how divine love found expression in a man and a woman once they were fully committed to doing His will. Surely, Joseph and Mary are to be commended, not only for discovering their own identity but also for rendering a great performance that prevented the curtain from prematurely falling on the stage of human need and salvation.

The love story of Joseph and Mary does more than stress the beauty and holiness of marriage; it also reveals a divine pathway of power for persons seeking to be successful in their quest for eternal living.

Not every story has such a beautiful ending. Not every person finds a proper place in the scheme of life's creation. Not every person is able to be, or cares to be, successful, or even to understand the reason for his or her success or failure. Not every person learns to be self-reliant or to trust others upon whom he must depend to compensate for his own weakness. Such persons are quick to ask, "Is there any such thing as unselfish love? Why should one love? Is love not merely a shortcut to selfishness? We may love others for free, but in so doing, do we not seek to satisfy our private needs to be expressive? Is it possible to obey the biblical command to 'Love thy neighbor as thyself'? Why are some people loved while others receive so little of this life's soul-searching virtue?"

During times of war, the soldiers living in communities near military bases and staging areas are sometimes ignored and considered socially unacceptable—even by the religious establishments in the area. I learned that military soldiers are not always welcome on holy ground. While training for the extreme and costly invasion of Japan, I attended a worship service at the First Church in Augusta, Georgia. There were some 300 civilians in attendance that Sunday morning in early March 1945. I was in for a rude awakening. Not one parishioner spoke to me before the service began or after the service was concluded. Even though every other seat in the sanctuary seemed to be taken, no one sat within three spaces of me. Perhaps that explained the absence of other military personnel in the congregation. I was the only person there who was wearing a military uniform, and I realized I was out of place. I had the feeling that those fine folks did not want their people associating with those heathens out there at Camp Gordon. They treated me as if I had the plague.

The pastor was being semifriendly while standing at the door of the church as those in attendance filed out to leave. There was a short break in the line as I made my exit. I could not help but realize that he was of the age to be a member of the armed forces, but I knew that his ministerial credentials excused him. At the time, he briefly made a comment or two concerning vague matters of interest, but nothing was said about my being welcome there. I believe that he was really thinking, *What are you doing here?* Our discussion was quickly terminated as other people drew near the door of the sanctuary. That was my first and last visit to that church. I have never heard of a group of people being sued for religious malpractice, but there are exceptions to every rule.

I felt more comfortable worshiping on base with my own kind rather than trying to find an outside church where I would feel accepted and nurtured. I felt that the message of love, hope, and comfort was reserved for those who perhaps were not in as much need of sustenance as was I at the time. I had never been more than 100 miles from home, and the people I knew were largely those I had known all of my life. But here I was seeking solace in a church away from home. However, instead of acceptance and affirmation, I found only resentment and rejection.

That experience introduced me to the idea that the soldier only becomes an "angel of mercy" while climbing a far distant mountain on Iwo Jima or struggling through the steaming jungles of Burma, India, New Guinea, or Viet Nam. His human credentials are most commonly accepted as he slugs out another yard of ground on the battlefields of Europe or gradually perishes in the filth and starvation of a prisoner of war camp in Germany, Japan, and other hostile countries where helpless victims have been confined in recent decades. There, he is out of touch with the protected and the uninvolved. And, as soon as the conflict is over, the home front that hailed his victory will unite to repress his efforts to establish himself in a society of equals.

Is it necessary for people to suffer before they can appreciate comfort and community? Does poverty have an important lesson to teach, concerning wealth? Such considerations were echoed in my mind as I recalled some past statements made by one long-time dweller in the city of Memphis, Tennessee, where I resided at that time. He was a newspaper reporter. He said, "We had a great city as long as it was composed of our original city folk. It began to disintegrate as country people and war veterans began to flock to our area at the end of the World War II." It was hard for me to retain a peaceful composure after hearing those words.

Surely, he spoke for himself, but his assessment of facts was not borne out of practical results. While living and working in Memphis, I came to realize that many of the medical doctors, legal scholars, school professors, as well as other skilled workers, came from the rural areas of the surrounding states.

It was not until the migration of skilled and semiskilled workers to the trade sectors of the city that new malls and shopping centers begin to pop up in various sections and vast numbers of shoppers came to town. Hospitals began to be enlarged, and specialized medical treatment expanded. Universities experienced large enrollments, producing skilled employees to bolster a concentrated and stagnated physical, social, and intellectual economy. Even with such progress, the city was reported, by a recent scientific study, to be 20 years behind many other cities of similar size and opportunity.

These considerations should cause a person to ask, "Are people our business, or is business our people? Do we only need others as long as they complement our personal needs? Or, do we accept persons for whom and what they are—equals in a world of unexhausted opportunities and possibilities for human betterment?" I think it is safe to say that the artificial doors we create to keep us apart are just as real as those created and constructed in the carpenter's shop.

Chapter Eight

Patience Is Prudent

To participate in progress is a part of the journey of faith. And patience helps to keep this movement going. To be reconciled to God is to affirm divine will. Woe is usually the result of the fragmentation of that which is good for all concerned. After each adventure, there comes a time when it is important to reflect on the circumstances at hand and determine how results could have been of a more positive nature.

People are largely governed by what they think about life. Some people live for the present, caring only for what they can get and enjoy today. They make no provision for disaster or sickness that may come in a few months or years; hence, when disaster comes upon them, they are wholly unprepared for it and are apt to blame God for what is, in fact, their own negligence.[10]

When a person loses his will to be patient, he has lost the ability to daily direct his course of constant living. Be it a king in a castle or a beggar seeking alms on the street, when a person loses the attitude of expectancy, personal survival becomes a chore, too monumental to successfully manage. It is then that he becomes mentally blinded by the stress factors that have defeated his sense of expected accomplishments. A person's search for success or happiness must be balanced with his willingness to pause and give his personal energies a rest from routine labors.

When a person finds himself thrust into new environments, it is important for that person to be able to retain a positive sense of self. This identification comes in many forms. Often, the simple experiences and events of the past revisit us with renewed vigor. To recall a long-ago visit with an old friend can do wonders for a weary and troubled mind. Revisiting the old home place can bring the past and present a little closer together. When it is impossible to renew old friendships, it is helpful to replace them with new friends and current experiences. Such socialization can take many forms and fashions and can bring about a transition from the "par-for-the-course" situation.

I often referred to our C. O. as "a good soldier's friend, but a bad soldier's misery." Captain Bauer was 53 years old and had been in the Army since he was 19 years old. One afternoon, I entered the prison office and took a seat as Captain Frank J. Bauer and Desk Sergeant Clevenger continued a casual conversation. It was their discussion, and I took no part in their verbal exchange until some time later. The captain finally made a statement that allowed me to respond. He said, "One thing I have always prided myself in is that I could almost always tell a person's age." It became obvious to me that I was about to put the good man behind the eight ball! I commented, "Well, Captain, how old do you think I am?"

He replied in a very forthright manner, "Reid, you are thirty."

I said, "Sir, you have missed my age by almost 10 years."

This gentleman replied quickly, "Reid, you need a vacation."

I readily agreed and replied, "Yes, Sir, I do, don't I?"

Edward Buehler and I had worked together for some time, but we had never had a social outing together. Edward was a very likable fellow—good moral character and very dependable in his position of military employment. Late one evening, Edward and I decided that the time had come to take a few hours off and enjoy a trip into Baguio, some 30 miles into the highest mountain in the Philippine Islands. I decided to heed the advice of my superior, Captain Bauer, who advised me to take a short break from my duties.

Baguio was called "The Garden Spot of the Orient." The city—located on the East Coast of the South China Sea—was a unique contrast to San Fernando. Our station was hot, humid, and populated with unwanted intruders—monkeys that roamed the tops of the abundant coconut and banana trees that were nearby. There were also huge scorpions that sometimes prowled inside the roof of our sleeping quarters. Practically all of the best public buildings and dwelling houses had been either destroyed or heavily damaged during World War II. Consequently, most of the civilians were living in small houses that had been hastily constructed from split bamboo poles and covered with tropical grass for a roof. Some of the stone buildings were being temporarily repaired, but the whole area was still in shambles.

When leaving San Fernando to go to Baguio, it was as if one was leaving one world and entering another. The first 10 miles of the route were over level roadways, but the war-damaged blacktop road covered the rest of the distance to the mountains. I put the jeep in four-wheel drive and began to grind out the up-and-around unbelievable curves and hills. At night, when descending from Baguio, I could look straight down beneath our location and view the lights from other vehicles on the same winding passageway. It was like looking out the window of an airplane and viewing a lighted farmhouse in the distance. When nearing the end of the upward journey, I could watch the rain clouds float by. The entire trip was an experience of a lifetime. I had traveled this route two or three times before, but I think this was Buehler's first encounter with this rugged portion of nature.

When we entered the mountain province, the air suddenly became cool and fresh—no smell of pollution or stagnation. Flowers were growing abundantly. No banana stalks or coconut trees could be seen, but large pine trees decorated the mountain resort in every direction. I remember two roadside signs that were near the entrance to the mountains. One read: Here Lies the Body of Harry White. He Wanted to Turn Left. But He Turned Right. The other billboard was designed to be a warning to the travelers: So Many Killed—So Many Wounded—So Many Still Missing.

Beyond almost every turn, there was a recently composed dirt door to the enemy's dugout (or pillbox) that had been constructed by bulldozers. This was also the enemy's tomb. They gave travelers an eerie feeling when passing by them in the darkness of the night.

The trip to Baguio defied description. A person had to experience it to believe the impact it made. When one sought to shed the rigid life-style of San Fernando for a short visit into another world, this was the place to go, and soldiers from all over the islands went there for rest and relaxation.

Buehler (military personnel usually call one another by their last names) and I completed our outing by having our evening meal in a large, three-story stone building, part of which was being used as a public restaurant. Before I relate information about our dinner, I need to mention a scene from six months earlier on the Baguio road. While serving as a military policeman, my partner and I came upon the first section of the lower drive and observed a young civilian man walking and leading approximately 40 grown dogs. I stopped our jeep nearby and inquired, "Joe, where are you going with all of those dogs?"

He replied, "I'm going to Baguio."

My curiosity was not satisfied, so I asked the native another question, "What are you going to do with all of those dogs?"

This young Filipino man became very specific, "I'm going to sell them. They bring much money. They make very good food." That inquiry ended, and I thought little more about the subject for some 40 years.

Buehler and I entered the restaurant and took seats near the wall next to the front of the dining room. Our table was covered with a neat white tablecloth, white napkins, and "the works." The waiter came around and handed us a menu. He was wearing a large white apron that covered a major portion of the front of his body. My eyes focused on a listing of barbecue and fries. My friend said, "I'll have the same."

After our waiter left, we viewed our immediate surroundings. We were in a large room with many tables; however, very few of the diners were there strictly for the purpose of eating. I remember saying to my companion, "Man, this is something. I haven't been exposed to such social call since stateside. This is certainly a change of venue." My partner was in full agreement with me. Our meal was pretty good—regular-cut fries, and the meat was "pulled," no bones. I suppose we both felt as if we had finally reconnected with a past life-style that had been more enjoyable, and we had somewhat succeeded in our efforts to become more sociable in a strange world.

Is it not strange how often time plays tricks on us or even helps to educate us to something we had overlooked long ago? Some 40 years after that evening meal in the mountain city of Baguio, I was returning to my home from another nearby city and traveling on Interstate 40. The traffic was not heavy, and I cruised along in my pickup truck. My mind was casually reviewing some scenes from many years ago, when I was jolted into an alert awareness. I abruptly began to speak to myself. (I suppose when one is speaking to himself, he may say what is on his mind!) *Evidently, you are the most stupid person in the whole United States of America. You knew there were no hogs in the Philippine Islands. You knew what that man said on the highway that day as he slowly moved his livestock on the way to market.* Well, I suppose if the barbecue were going to kill me, it would have done so before now.

As I reflect on that outing, in which Buehler and I sought to improve our social status, I cannot say whether we succeeded or failed. I sometimes wonder if it also took him 40 years to reconcile the ambiguity between innocence and ignorance! There is one thing for sure, as my partner and I left that restaurant, we did not know that we were giving true human embodiment to the term, "doggie bags!"

Endurance

Possessing an enduring nature is characteristic of a person who is dedicated to succeeding. It is a quality of the disciplined effort necessary for ultimate victory in a worthwhile endeavor. The will to endure provides evidence that a person is competing with his best self, and not with others. Ignatius of Loyola was just such a person. He was playing a game of ball with his fellow students when someone seriously asked, What would each of them do if he suddenly discovered that he had only 20 minutes left to live?"

All agreed they would rush quickly to the church for prayer—all except Ignatius, who answered, "I would finish my ballgame."

Patience is a strong motivator of effort, the guardian of accomplishment, and the companion of hope. Surely, the testimony of every thoughtful person joins that of the Psalmist who said, "I would have fainted unless I had believed to see the goodness of the Lord in the land of the living" (Psalm 27:13).

Yes, sitting down and charting one's course for life is a major undertaking. One may choose a vocation, but success within his program of life rises to the surface only as circumstances and events are effectively dealt with on an on-going basis. "Faith is our readiness to receive the costly gift of new life that God offers to us in the crucified and risen Lord."[11]

When we begin to walk through the valleys of the shadow of life and the uncertainties of living, we either find something to hold on to or else perish along the way. "We must get beyond ourselves. We must find our wills caught up in some larger, wider purpose than our own self-interest."[12]

The emphasis of Christianity becomes very real at this point. Its nature of new beginnings or small beginnings should not be underestimated. Christian theology not only provides direction for commitment and stability but it also admonishes us to accept the blame for our own failures and mistakes. It is flexible enough to make room for the unavoidable and unintentional, yet it seeks to inform the believer that sins and conflict should never hold the final word over a helpless victim.

Not only must we strive to persevere, but we must also encourage others to succeed, and we must share in their happiness when positive attainments have been reached. This is not as unselfish as it may appear, since sharing hope with others employs a twofold effort. First, it aids the welfare and strengthens the cause of a person in need. Second, benevolent giving of self strengthens the charitable spirit of the one who gives unselfishly. "It is the nature of compassion not only to enter into the suffering of another but to take steps to relieve the suffering."[13]

In order to share the plight of others, we must be willing to share their frustrations, rejoice with them in their victories, and be sensitive to their needs. There comes a time when discussions of right and wrong, humor and sadness, suggestions and observations are not enough. To such reasoning, the sensitive person will stop and ask, "So what?" If a person is to be very helpful with the decisions of others regarding the solution of personal problems and the prevention of tragedy, then advice must include specific information and encouragement.

On February 2, 1993, I attended a seminary class at the Methodist Hospital in Memphis, Tennessee. Chaplain Jesse Moore quoted one distressed person who said, "The Church is less effective than the police force when dealing with my condition. The Church must help a weak person build up his immune system. This is best done by serving

as an agent of reconciliation instead of an agency of condemnation and rejection."

I gave the following advice and encouragement to a
group of young people who were graduating from high
school the next day:

I strongly disagree with the following statement
that I often hear made during graduation cere-
monies: "You are now going out into the world."
You are already in the world. You have been caught
up in the business of living for seventeen or eigh-
teen years. You have already won many victories.
Your life-temperaments are already set. You may
make some adjustments, but what you become in-
tellectually, morally, and spiritually depends
largely upon who you are, and what you are today.
You are simply continuing to seek identity and give
effective expression to your individuality in a constantly changing world.

Today, you bear the good names and many
good fortunes of your parents, peers, teachers, and
others, but your life is your own. We wish to con-
gratulate all of the people who have given so much
to undergird your moral and mental characteristics, your social graces, and your stability. No
person can afford to live on his or her past record
or on his or her present popularity. Retirement
from business is a part of our way of life, but spiritual, social, and mental retirements are blights
upon the cause of humanity. You must have faith.
"But add to your faith diligence and virtue and to
virtue knowledge."

Cultivate your faith. Test and try it. Do not be

slow to believe that which offers helpful possibilities. Do not be afraid to doubt. Examine your supreme values frequently. Allow them to be tested in the light of Christian truth and hope. Remain firm in your support of religious issues that have been validated by past experience. Be aware that many voices will call out and seek your recognition and response, but be ever mindful that evil calls, as well as righteousness, and you are the one to determine the difference.

You will be extended invitations to sell your birthright for a few dollars or a more elevated position among your peers. Some voices will bargain with you for your future happiness and for your spiritual security. Listen with care and make your choices based upon what you deem to be appropriate for all concerned. Be mindful that there will be times when your only solace will be in your awareness that you have done your very best to succeed. Let all of us remember the words of Lord Brougham, "Education makes a person easy to lead, but difficult to drive; easy to govern, but impossible to enslave."

Success is an elusive endeavor demanding constant search even when progress remains obscured by repeated failure. Attainment is not the result of a single decisive battle or a brief sudden accomplishment. It is more like a marathon of competing athletes where the greatest satisfaction is derived, not from winning the race, but rather by displaying faithful and adequate energies in the process of competition. A few years ago, I had the occasion to visit a friend I had not seen for some time. She was very excited about the annual Boston Marathon. She never once mentioned the possibility of winning, but the thrill of competing was very interesting to her.

I am becoming more aware that a basic ingredient for successful human interaction is to go to others when they do not come to us. But this is no small task. By our very nature, we are somewhat timid. Many people do not appear that way, but offering oneself to individuals and groups on a personal basis is risky business. Even the most arrogant and seemingly unlikable person is seldom as forthright as his outward appearance suggests. Yet, each would-be friend must ask the question, "Am I willing to run the risk of being hurt in order to aid the welfare of a prospective friend?"

One definition of patience is "long suffering under provocation." To exercise patience means to listen to our neighbor's call for help, even when his cries are deafening to our ears. One of the instructors at Pastor's School at Lambuth College in Jackson, Tennessee, made the following statement, which is worthy of further consideration: "Do not abandon the people you [attract]. When the glitter and glamour are over, stick with them." This advice was given to pastors, encouraging them to find places of usefulness and involvement for new members in the church and not to consider church-alignment as being the ultimate goal of Christian evangelism.

The Christian church needs to be more employed in the creation of a more just world of love, joy, peace, and spiritual prosperity. Saints are not human forms of decoration but rather souls trying to decorate their unattractiveness with usefulness. Thus, we need to be careful, lest patience be reduced to indifference or laziness. It is very easy for the membership of a church or a segment of its membership to get off in its own little corner and think it all begins and ends there. The future belongs to the faithful people who have recognized the never-ending need for Christian stewardship in the affairs of all persons.

One day, my oldest brother, Noel, asked me if I had ever held a funeral service for a murderer. I answered, "Yes."

My brother's reply was, "What do you say at such a time?"

I responded, "Well, Noel, I say about the same thing at each and every memorial service, and that is: 'But for the grace of God, there go I.'"

I like Jesus' teaching in Luke's Gospel, concerning personal responsibility for one's neighbor: "What man of you having an hundred sheep, if he lose one of them doth not leave the ninety and nine in the wilderness, and go after that which is lost, until he find it?" (Luke 15:4). The church of tomorrow will be the one that portrays a patient and constant effort of "reaching out in new ways, with relevant words and deeds toward the people of God in most desperate need of the sustaining and revitalizing power of a resurrected faith."[14]

The Church needs to be more aggressive in affirming a practical and workable faith. Many people are impatient with Christianity because they believe civilization is doomed to failure. The Gospel was born in an unfriendly environment, and it has never outgrown its origin. But a resistance to truth is not a true characterization of the New Testament era or its effort to be a blessing to those in assorted needs.

A young minister was assigned to a church located in

an area reputed to have vice. He was determined to bring about a state of moral reform. And, for some time, with the aid of some churchmen, there was noticeable success. But then, they dropped their resistance to many of the community ills. When asked why, he replied, "The good people got tired of being good before the bad people got tired of being bad."

Patience is the product of conscience, conviction, and commitment. It is a characteristic of an integrated faith, determination, and reconciliation of personal values. The importance of patience is profoundly stated in the Bible: "Better is the end of a thing than the beginning there of and the patient in spirit is better than the proud in spirit" (Ecclesiastes 7:8).

The legitimate acceptance of oneself conditions an individual to accept her limited perfection. There is a real sense in which "going on to perfection," the Christian theology of John Wesley, the founder of the Methodist movement, applies to the whole of positive personal effort and conduct.

A large number of people have identity problems. And, to complicate the matter further, many are forever changing their self-images, behavioral patterns, and responses in hopes of coinciding with the varied dispositions and desires of others with whom they come in contact. We pretend to be actors (and we actually are), but in reality, we are seeking to be worthy of each social encounter. However, planned dramatization of self is best left to the professional actors whose business it is to entertain audiences and please individuals. For entertainment, this is wholesome and good; in religion and real life, it is a tragedy. A person cannot be everything to everyone and remain true to his best self.

Patience Is Prudent

While serving as pastor of the First United Methodist Church in Henderson, Tennessee, it became necessary on a particular occasion for me to practice patience to the fullest extent. On December 30, 1979, I arose to preach a sermon to a congregation that nearly filled the sanctuary. At that moment, a middle-aged man, who was a stranger to all who were present, made his way to the front and took a seat directly in front of the pulpit. After a very short interval, he removed a badly blood-soiled handkerchief from his pocket and began to wave it back and forth in an effort to catch my attention. My first thought was, *Has he mistaken the setting of this worship service with that of a Spanish bullfighting arena, or is he simply a mean person intent on making a mockery of my message?* I later discovered that he was a patient (without leave) from a hospital in another city. But at the time, I could only wonder what the reason was for this strange and unexpected contribution to the morning worship service. Never before had I experienced the waving of a red flag under such circumstances. This demanded full and complete concentration on the matter at hand. One person who was present suggested that the man be encouraged to return each Sunday because his presence had actually improved the quality of my speaking.

Patience amounts to disciplined anticipation. He who cultivates this virtue expects ultimate victory and seeks to be content until it comes. No person should be resolved to await failure but should rather seek to prevent it. Yet, we are an impatient people—impatient to grow up and become adults and restless about our constant advancement toward senior-citizen status. The hasty person is very apt to reflect the frustration of the psalmist, who cried out in desperation, "O Lord, how long wilt thou hide thy face from me?" (Psalm 13:1).

Prolonged illness can cause great anxiety, and it is hard to tolerate. Possessing a positive faith during such times of distress is very helpful, but faith for any person is never limitless. A person may become critical of religion and complain that deliverance from adversities is deceptive and undependable. An ill person needs to be aware that he does not hold a monopoly on such a state of perplexity. Jesus said, "I have yet many things to say to you, but you cannot bear them now" (John 16:12).

Patience teaches us that the development of good is not confined to that which is good, pleasant, and comfortable. This is a hard lesson to learn and an even harder theory to employ. But the patient bearing of burdens produces refinement of character and personality and gives needed strength that may be shared with others.

A minister-friend of mine related to me a conversation that he once had with a terminally ill parishioner. It was common knowledge that the woman would not live more than a few days longer. The patient shared this fact and spoke freely of her impending death. The only encouragement that she accepted was the advice of her pastor. "Your bearing of this burden may well be the best ministry to people of weaker faith that you have ever been able to perform." It is in times of quiet assurance that we are most apt to believe, as Paul did, that "in everything God works for good with those who love him" (Romans 8:28).

The loss of patience results in moral and spiritual frustration. I have known many Christians whose work in the church involved anxious endeavors to move the Christian cause forward, but whose energies were depleted by casual responses to their zealous prodding. People who go about the business of practicing Christianity with much vigor and haste, as though they had to make up for lost time spent outside the religious community, soon burn themselves out, because Christianity cannot be consumed; one has to be consumed by it.

I remember well one such man whom I once served as pastor. This man worked hard to carry out the programs of the church and would extend no small amount of public criticism toward those who took a more leisurely and constant view of congregational ministry. Today, some 12 years later, he does not attend or support his former church, but most of those about whom he complained at the time are still loyal practitioners of the faith.

The Apostle Paul was an impatient man. His Roman background and former hatred and persecution of Christians set the stage for a mental and spiritual battle following his conversion. Some of his theological teachings had to be reconciled to the teachings of Jesus. Perhaps, one of the most noticeable considerations was that of Christ's impending return to earth after his death and resurrection. Paul held the opinion that it was not expedient for persons to marry and establish homes and families because they would not be around long enough for this to happen. As time went on, however, Paul was compelled to be more patient in his approach to matters of life, living, and salvation.

Paul came to possess and affirm a more patient disposition. He began to realize that, "Like the ocean, life is too large for us to know all about it by direct experience. Our widely spaced islands of limited knowledge cannot answer the deep mysteries of life."[15] In I Corinthians 13, Paul acknowledges that we understand life as if it were a conglomeration of figments reflected by a mirror. "Today, we see in part, but, when the perfect comes, the imperfect will pass away" (1 Corinthians 13:10). "When faith runs thin we begin to ask for a sign for proof."[16]

When haste beats itself out trying to reconcile the eternal with the here and now, patience of mind and motive enter the picture with the announcement that "On the good ground are they, which in an honest and good heart, having heard the word, keep it, and bring forth fruits with patience" (Luke 8:15).

It seems to me that the saddest stories told are those about people who almost made it but failed. Little Byron Hall, who received a liver transplant at the children's hospital in Memphis a few months ago, almost recovered. I once held the funeral service for a helicopter crewman who was killed on his last combat mission over Viet Nam. One failing grade has prevented many college students from ever graduating. So many of life's greatest events have hung in the balance of success and failure.

Some 600,000 people died because the church was not consistent and patient in its ministry to humanity. Historians tell us that, to a large extent, the Civil War was a product of the church's failure to deal with the stressful issues of the day. At that time, members of the Methodist, Baptist, and Presbyterian denominations accounted for nearly 95 percent of the church members in America. The church lost its impact on the direction of the new nation because it could not decide what to do with the question of slavery.

History gives sad testimony to the high cost of giving up on the social and moral issues of society. When John Wesley told his preachers, "You have nothing to do but save souls," he never intended that the Christian Church should be indifferent to the assorted needs of people. He advocated salvation of the total person and complete life.

The loss of patience creates seepage of faith and a weakening of moral character. Being not far from peace is not the same thing as the enjoyment of dwelling in harmony with others and with oneself. Remaining not far from social success is not the same thing as sharing progressive human accomplishments. Being not far from loving thy neighbor as thyself is not as helpful to all concerned as feeling a true kinship and appreciation for one's neighbor. Being not far from a state of salvation does not give the satisfaction and security that comes with the assurance that a person has given complete dedication to the best he knows. The failure to remain faithful to prior commitments and accepted values creates weakness that hastens to grow more prolific in the mind of the person who has imposed upon his faith and squandered his rational composure.

A person can be near the borders of success yet be so far away. When there are yet things to be done for the betterment of all concerned, they should be done. Patience so often makes the difference between saying, "I almost succeeded in the accomplishment of my lifelong dreams," and saying, "My greatest desires have become a reality because I endured with hope, faith, and patience." Bishop Earl G. Hunt, Jr., said, "Thus each new morning should be a magic scroll; a parchment of reverent optimism."

Chapter Nine

Settling for Second Best

During no era of history can people expect to formulate a perfect society, but they should, rather, seek to construct a functional method of communication between the elements of opposition. There cannot be an elimination of all problems confronting individuals and groups, but advocating positive methods of dealing with adversity can do much to minimize public and private discomfort. There is no substitute for dialogue and the viewing of conditions from the position of one's adversary. Perhaps there is no better stance from which to view such a position than that of reflecting on these words from the Bible: "Do unto others as you would have them to do unto you."

Modern humanity should not take comfort, but enlightenment, from the fact that recorded history portrays human conduct to be more introverted than extroverted. For a classic example, we have only to note the conduct of Jesus' disciples prior to Pentecost. They were more concerned about their safety than they were concerned for the public good. "They had received the command to go share this news with the whole world. Yet . . . they had shut themselves up behind closed doors for fear of the people. They had the message the world needed, the only message that could cure the sin-hurt of the world and yet that message was closed in behind closed doors."[17]

The successful person is one who labors within the framework of his abilities and his opportunities. Often, the only difference between one person becoming a success and another becoming a failure is simply their abilities and willingness to cope with the tasks that cannot be altogether completed and conditions that cannot be eliminated. All of the disturbing noises of life cannot be silenced. Some must be endured.

A sensitive person will seek to determine the time and type of remedy that is appropriate for the occasion. This fact took on a real significance for me a few months ago when a friend and I shared a dormitory room while visiting a college campus. The door to our room was heavy and gave forth a disturbing squeak each time it was opened and closed. However, after I applied liquid detergent to its hinges, a person could enter and leave the room in complete silence. That is exactly what happened that very night. A thief entered and took our money without our discovering it until we needed cash to pay our bills the next day. Unknown to me, the door, which could not be locked, would have provided a perfect burglar alarm system.

Problems—which both trouble and challenge—tempt a person to lock the door of personal experience and throw away the key of effort, yet such a practice is characteristic of a person's weaker moments and is not symbolic of his most endurable nature.

George H. Morrison pointed out a great truth in one of his sermons: "The Bible lifts the veil for us a little, and we find there was compassion in it." There is a second truth that might well follow: If the same veil is once again lowered, we find that compassion has disappeared. But life is of such a nature that messages of hope and salvation may be extracted from events partially hidden behind the veils of imperfection, a troubled nature, and stressful living.

I used to watch ships that were anchored in the San Fernando Harbor of the Philippine Islands rush out to sea to avoid destruction by the sudden arrival of typhoons in the South China Sea. For these mighty units of human construction to survive the threat, they had to have space to roll and drift. To remain anchored in shallow waters would have meant sudden and complete destruction for these magnificent vessels that had survived the battles of World War II.

The importance of having a sense of preservation is a lesson that humanity has yet to learn well. As a universal people, we seem to spend more energy on correcting our mistakes than we spend on preventing them. But this is a luxury that has become too expensive for the welfare of all concerned. Why are we not content to be a good civilization, knowing full well that we shall never be perfect people? Why can we not realize that we are not called to be better than we are capable of being or more than we should be?

In a recent article in the *Commercial Appeal* newspaper (Memphis, Tennessee), Bessie Anderson Stanley quotes from a column by Ann Landers, and this conveys my most sincere sentiments:

To laugh often and much; to win the respect of intelligent people and the affection of children; to earn the appreciation of honest critics and endure the betrayal of false friends; to appreciate beauty; to find the best in others; to leave the world a little better place than we found it, whether by a healthy child, a garden patch, or a redeemed social condition; to know even one life breathed easier because you lived: This is to have succeeded.

I do not dare suggest that I am offering myself as an adequate example of the positive postulates that are mentioned in this book. I do, however, affirm them, and I extend degrees of effort to practice them, but I have not reached, nor will I ever reach, a state of perfection in matters of faith, fortitude, patience, and moral character. Nevertheless, I do exercise a degree of satisfaction in knowing that they are important to me, as well as to other sensitive persons.

I am not seeking to be content with second best, but rather, to use that which is until that which is better becomes a reality. For me, this is movement in the proper direction.

When it is chosen, rather than when it is accepted as an imposition, settling for less than the best is blight to personal character. Personal success quite often exceeds rational expectation. Though the Apostle Paul was often confused about his evaluation of himself, he does give us assistance in the understanding of our rightful selves. In Romans 12:3, Paul said, "For I say, through the grace given unto me, to every man that is among you, not to think of himself more highly than he ought to think; but to think soberly, according as God hath dealt to every man the measure of faith."

An individual should be happy to know that she could be a better person, not boasting of her weakness, but rejoicing in her possibilities. Several years ago, I heard a radio announcer tell an interesting story that happened while he was a youth in school: "I felt it would be cool to wear a pair of overalls and combat boots to school. But, because my friends laughed at me, I gave the clothes to a less fortunate boy and joined in the fun and mockery of him, who in turn, beat me up."

Accepting ourselves for who we are is no small task. Too many of our values are external in nature, which means that we seek to claim and possess rather than to give expression to virtues.

In his novel on fortitude, Walpole makes an interesting statement: "It isn't life that matters; it's the courage you bring to it." Knowledge and training are never enough. We are called upon to produce fruit worthy of the investments made in us. I have known many students who would like to have attended school for their entire lives, but the time came when they could no longer enjoy the security of saying, "I'm still preparing for my vocation."

Each person should give frequent and honest thought to the question, which is more honorable, to serve or to be served? Jesus gave much validity to the office of servitude when he said that a servant is not greater than his master. We must be willing to apply our personal efforts in appropriate fashion.

I knew a preacher who often claimed he had ills worse than did anyone else. If he were told a sad story, he would usually try to top it. While speaking to the departing parishioners at the door of the church one Sunday morning, he fell victim to his own deception. "Mrs. Jones," he said, "I have not seen you in church lately."

With surprised anxiousness, she replied, "I've been in the hospital. I had major surgery—a hysterectomy. It liked to have killed me!"

Her sympathetic pastor quickly replied, "Yes, I know

what you have been through. I once had that type of surgery. It was almost more than I could stand. I thought I would die. It was plain awful."

If doorways could speak, many and varied would be the messages proclaimed. The reason is very clear: that is where much of the action takes place and where we are most apt to happily say hello or sadly say good-bye.

There are times when second best is better than first choice. Not many people want a weakling for a friend or servant. When a person displays the attitude that he is wearing himself out for others, he will soon discover that he does not have anything others want or need. The same is true of social dialogue between two people. When one person becomes aware that he has discovered another person's most interesting secret, he may lose interest in the relationship, and then both may become disillusioned with an association that ceases to produce meaningfulness and enjoyment.

Freedom is not a combination of past restrictions and current privileges. It is the ability to begin anew without an exaggerated threat of failures or the depression of artificial enslavement. Helmut Thielicke, a German pastor, wrote of the tragedies that characterized the German church and its membership during World War II. Concerning the major social and theological problems of judgment and guilt, which serve to create estrangement in human relationships, he said, "And even when we cannot find a guilty party in some great or small misfortune, we invent one."[18]

Invented obstacles to happiness often prevent people from enjoying the good life that is available to them. The challenge "wake up and live" needs to be recited often by all of us. That would help us better appreciate the opportunity of living and enjoying life within the framework of individual abilities and experiences.

A few years ago, a friend and I spent the night on a farm during late winter. There was little evidence of spring; however, a warm rain came that night. The next morning was brightened by the sun's reflection upon our surroundings, especially upon a wet maple tree that did not shed its leaves after the frosts fell.

Charles was the first to awake. While looking out the window of our cabin, across a nearby field, he focused upon a wonderful sight and called out to me, "Wake up, Rip Van Winkle. We've slept too long. The dogwoods are in bloom."

Human experience is much like the leaves on a tree. Some people respond to the challenge and promise of a new and better life; others refuse to let go until the new sap has begun to flow with sure opportunity, pushing away the frostbitten stems of another season. Such people sacrifice a later joy of a fuller life.

Now and then, some person comes along, walks into the compartments of our lives, and brings a lively spirit and a social freshness with him. One is fortunate to meet such a person. To know this sort of a person is to love him; to be separated from him is to open a void in life that takes more than time and circumstance to fill.

My brother, William T. Reid, was a person such as this. Prior to his death on November 13, 1992, at the age of 74, he made extensive plans for his departure from this life. One such preparation was the inscription on his grave marker. It read: I loved music, people, and nature. This is an indication of his personal attitude toward life, which enabled him to aid the lives of other people.

For Terry, life was so much larger than death, and he refused to allow his impending death to mar its significance. He lived life to the hilt, and he died without complaining. He suffered from a gradual disintegration of his physical faculties for nearly a year and finally succumbed to acute leukemia. During his ordeal, the nearest he came to complaining was to say, "I'm tired of taking all of these shots without getting any better."

Terry loved and enjoyed his family, his church, his profession of Federal Soils Conservationist, and his community. He would go out of his way to speak to isolated people who were sitting on benches around the court-square in Decaturville, Tennessee. One day I said to him, "You act as if you own this courthouse here in the city."

He replied, "Most of these people around here seem to think I do."

Terry loved to travel—not so much for the miles involved but for the enjoyment of meeting people along the way. During the summer preceding his death, Terry strongly encouraged his wife Alice, Christine and me, and our brother Roland and his wife Ann to join him on an overseas cruise. When I indicated it would not be possible for Christine and me to take the voyage, he said, "It may be later than you think. . . . It may be later than you think." It was. He never made that journey. But a few days before the scheduled departure, he made another one—one that would last forever.

My brother had the very best of medical and professional care. For some time, he made a weekly journey from his home in Parsons, Tennessee, to the Vanderbilt Clinic in Nashville. According to his attending physician at the clinic, "Four weeks were added to his life-span." On one occasion, I drove him there for his appointment. The

100 miles traveled that early morning will forever be stamped in my memory. I had come to realize he was a very sick man, but never did I realize his days were quickly coming to an end.

I was driving his new car. The sun came up bright and clear, and we were sipping hot coffee in the early morning. In a casual but specific voice, Terry said, "The medical profession can now pinpoint with a great deal of accuracy the outcome of my type of illness, but you know, I have always had a tendency to take this sort of thing in a light-hearted fashion. I have no regrets. I have had a full, interesting life." Terry's attention moved from his illness to the order of the moment. "My, this is such a beautiful day! What a nice day to travel."

Terry always had a ready ear for the other person's story. He would never leave someone emotionally stranded by telling a crude joke. He made an effort to lead every conversation toward wholesome thoughts. He met every person with a degree of excitement and an expectation of social enjoyment. He made it a habit to speak to people he did not know and showed an interest in the personal welfare of all of his associates.

When Terry died, the floral arrangements overflowed the space in both the chapel and the church, and a large amount of money was donated to his church, the First United Methodist Church of Parsons, Tennessee. During his life, he remembered others, and other people honored his considerate nature with their memorial gifts. He will long be remembered in the way his pastor, who conducted the memorial service, described him: "He was a party on wheels."

In order to facilitate his enjoyment of socialization, Terry shared his lodge with others. Many and varied were the parties enjoyed at his place. Church groups, civic and professional groups, United Methodist youth groups, and others often enjoyed this spacious and comfortable facility. The house was divided into two parts. One side contained the living quarters, kitchen, bath, fireplace, and a sitting room (which also served as a place to store and play his extensive music collection). A sheltered patio floor accounted for the other half of the lodge. This was located on a rise and faced the lake. This part was used for dancing, cooking out, and just plain old talking.

Today, the lodge remains quiet. Since Terry's death, there has been no cookout, music, or social event at the lodge. Not only do most members of Terry's immediate family reside in other towns but also that type of celebration has been placed on hold.

Some time ago, I drove along a nearby highway, remembering this place in its previous days. It happened to be a cold day as I thought about the recreation area of his place called "The Cabin." Now, only the cold wind blows across that floor of fond memories. Yet, I am mindful that unique warmth of heart abounds to erase much of the sadness of a chapter in our lives that now lies closed.

I write this not only from the point of view of a brother who lost a brother but also to express a sentiment that so many people share. I think of Terry on a daily basis. I usually re-examine my memories with a degree of sadness, but I end each such episode of pondering with a quiet and sensitive laugh because that is the way he lived, and that is the philosophy of life he embraced. Take and use the best; do that which makes you comfortable; do not fall victim to your low or depressed states of personal experience.

Surely the closing of the door to Terry's life opened

many others that will remain open for years to come. In the words of my older relative, "We have worn out two decades of people, and we have started on the third. We like to entertain and to be entertained."

Earlier in this writing, I spoke of people of history who had passed through the old train-depot-station door, now a part of Terry's lodge. There are many people who now say, "Terry stands tall on that list of unusual travelers who, over the years, passed through its portals." Terry is gone, but he left enough of himself with us to aid our journeys, as along the roadway of life we go. After all, that is what life is all about. Yes, this is a beautiful day. We must make a safe and happy trip. Maybe if my brother had met Robert Sikes, he would have convinced him to embrace life at its best.

I think Terry's philosophy of life was something like this: When one door closes behind you, open the one that lies ahead because that is where the greatest treasures of life currently abound.

Chapter Ten

Looking in Both Directions

Just as every veteran does, I had to go through a period of adjustment after my discharge from the military service. The war had been over for a year, but walking out of one life into another took a degree of conditioning of both mind and spirit.

I soon became aware of persons who were willing to aid me in my efforts. Such help comes in a variety of fashions and people, both formal and informal.

Noel, my eldest brother, served me quite well at this juncture of my life-travels. Perhaps he never knew it, but his personal stability provided a degree of security for me. He helped me to get my sights focused on the future. He was always patient when listening to me tell my tales of woe. Our work together on the farm helped me to regain a sense of community spirit and purpose. Of the six sons in our family, Noel was the only one who didn't serve in the armed forces, but he served the home front quite well. He never said so, but I sometimes wondered if Papa didn't consider Noel's largest fault to be that of being a Baptist.

Noel and Frances had been married about three years before I became a soldier in the United States Army. I was away for nearly two years and had not spent much time with them for some five years. Being with them was a good experience for me. Noel and I enjoyed not only our time working together but also the time we spent together in other activities. There was perhaps one exception that he did not enjoy too well.

In those days, there were not many tractors being used on farms in our community. We used mule teams for our source of farm power. Driving mules was much harder than driving a tractor. Late one evening, after we had fed our livestock for the night, we were on our way to our houses for the evening meal. We were hearty eaters as well as hard workers. Both Christine and Frances will vouch for that. Frances owned a half-gallon ice cream freezer. Quite often, our wives would treat us to homemade ice cream for dessert. We had not realized that we had been eating more than our share of the ice cream. It was sort of embarrassing when this was discovered. The ladies said later that they seldom got enough. Christine developed a bright idea. "Frances, let us make ourselves a full freezer of cream when they are not present and eat until our heart's content." They did. When we arrived, they appeared to be sick. I can still remember the sight of my nearly nauseated wife when we came into the dining room. They were almost ready to call a doctor. Those two women had consumed almost half a gallon of ice cream!

On that particular evening, Noel and I were approaching his backyard and observed a very large dog entering his hen house. Noel said, "Yonder is that dog that's been tearing up my hens' nests and getting my eggs." There happened to be a heavy-duty walking stick lying there at his feet. He grabbed that weapon and exclaimed, "I am going to give that dog a whipping and break him from his worrisome habit. When I step inside the building

behind him, I want you to slam the door and latch it."
This I did, and the activity behind the closed door began
in haste. This arrangement was in force for only a short
time. From the outside, I could not decide who was winning the contest.

My brother began to admonish me, "Open the door,
Russell, open the door!" I did, but not as fast as he wanted
me to. I was having a little fun of my own. When I did
open the door, Noel was the first one out. His face was as
white as a bed sheet, and he exclaimed, "Man, that thing
will eat a fellow up!"

I do not think I was trying to repay him for an earlier
statement he made to me, but the thought did cross my
mind. At that time, I was home on furlough before shipping overseas. I related to Noel that I was on my way to
join forces for the invasion of Japan and that the possibility of my returning home alive was very slim. He replied
by saying that I was just scared. I replied, "After what I've
just gone through in the state of Georgia, I'm not fearful at
all; I just don't want to die this young."

Noel just didn't understand the seriousness of the situation. He did not know the United States military had already suffered more than 300,000 casualties and was
expecting 90 percent of our invading forces to be lost
when the battle began on the shores of Japan. There was
still heated debate in the halls of the war department in
Washington regarding whether or not the American people
would stand for nearly a million more to be added to that
number. The battle that was to come a month later was referred to as the "Battle of Armageddon."

So, while the short contest was going on in the hen
house, I reasoned, *Big man, since you are so capable of
handling anything unafraid, I'll give you a little extra*

time to demonstrate your defense. Noel did not get mad at me, but when he came out, he breathed a sigh of relief. It is strange what brothers will do to each other. Underneath all of that love and appreciation for each other, there may remain a small degree of competition.

Noel later became an excellent house builder. He built friendships as well as houses. He was very determined that people received full measure for what they paid. From his sickbed, he was able to tell me how to build my house.

My brother was very loyal to his family, his church, and all people in general. The people he worked for, in turn, had great confidence in him.

One of the most interesting stories he ever related to me was something that happened while he played college football under legendary coach, Bear Bryant, at Union University in Jackson, Tennessee. His two roommates were not from West Tennessee and referred to him as "country boy." They developed the habit of rushing into their room and slapping, punching, and ridiculing him. Noel said, "One day, I just caught the two dudes and squeezed them together until they nearly popped. They never did bother me anymore."

When Noel died, I was invited to make a few remarks during his memorial service. I said, in part, "Noel never had the time or opportunity to be a child. He has always been a man." His memory and inspiration is very real to us all. Transitional aids come in assorted packages, and when they leave, further adjustments in life must be made.

College and the Ministry

My next 13 years were spent farming, operating a small country store, and attending church. Many Sundays,

Christine, Jean, and I would have lunch with Mama and Papa, and after an afternoon visit, we would return to our modest home, some 10 miles away, and wait for the next workday to come.

The greatest event during this 13-year period was the birth of our daughter, who became our pride and joy and, to this very day, still is. Other family members have come to join us, but no one has taken the place of Jean.

If high school was an awakening, then college was a shock. My ministerial duties began at the same time that I began my first semester in college. I have often said, "Somebody was crazy for giving me that church appointment, and I was crazy for accepting it." My re-entry into the pursuit of an education followed a most unusual course.

Perhaps the following account will help to explain the dean of admissions' apparent reservation to accept me as a full-time student. I was 35 years of age, Christine and I had been married for 13 years, and our daughter Jean was 10 years of age. My scholastic credentials at the time were a high school diploma—obtained by passing a graduate equivalency exam—and a certificate for having passed a civil service examination (to my surprise, I ranked eighth highest in the group of prospective state employees who took the exam with me).

I felt fear at the time I enrolled but joy when I graduated four and one-half years later. As Dean Whybrew—who is still the dean of admissions—passed through the reception line honoring graduating seniors, he said to me, "Russell, there are many students graduating here tomorrow simply because you are. You would not give up, so neither would they."

My last appointment before retirement was in a

town—the county seat—near where I was reared. After being at that church for a very short time, a man with whom I had attended one year of school in Brownsville, Tennessee, asked me to give an account of my education credentials. Twice before, in official meetings at the church, he had indirectly approached the subject of my ministerial education. I just turned the matter aside. It was an aggravating experience for me.

During a third such approach, he asked me what year I had graduated from the Haywood County High School (he knew that I had not graduated from there). I gave him a specific answer, "I received my high school diploma under the authority of the American School in Chicago. I earned a Bachelor of Arts degree from Lambuth College and a Master of Divinity degree from the Cumberland Presbyterian Seminary in Memphis, Tennessee. Marshall, does my answer satisfy your inquiry?"

Yet, I will hasten to say my troublesome adjustment to college was largely countered by one of my professors, who was in a position to send a college graduate to Duke Divinity School with all expenses paid. He offered that scholarship to me; I had to graciously decline the offer.

Another professor, Mr. Billy P. Exum, for whom I had great respect, and whose friendship I shall cherish for the rest of my life, also made a generous offer to me. He placed a full scholarship paper on my desk and said, "Russell, take a look at this. Will you go to the University of Florida, get a PhD, and come back and teach sociology at Lambuth College?"

I replied, "Mr. Exum, you do not know how much I appreciate your confidence in me, but you know why I am here. I must continue my preparation for the Christian ministry. I am compelled to say no."

The great man responded, "I understand."

I want to underscore the words, "the great man under-stood." They are very characteristic of Mr. Exum. He was an attorney.

Many a day while in class, I would look at him and ask myself how he could work for a college professor's salary when he could be practicing law and earning so much more money. The answer was simple. He believed that he was doing what he should have been doing, and he seemed to be completely happy teaching school.

Mr. Exum had an excellent memory and another unique ability. It was somewhat strange, but if one gave undivided attention to him, he was able to instill an ability to learn in that person. On one occasion, I informed him in a casual sense that I had discovered his uniqueness. He did not say a word. He just looked at me and grinned. He was very instrumental in pulling me out of an intellectual slump, and he aided me in graduating from college. I owe him something. What a man he was! What a teacher he was!

If college was an awakening for me, seminary became an illumination. It was truly a time of transition. It be-came a turning point in my road of life. I tried not to lose sight of where I had been, but new awakenings reached the surface of my awareness. After college, I thought semi-nary would be a breeze, but again, I came to realize that there were still many questions for which I did not have the answers. It was another world to me and required dis-ciplines yet to be discovered.

A segment of the Memphis Annual Conference of min-isters was in session in Jackson, Tennessee, for a specific purpose. Our current conference administrator, H. Ellis

Finger, had driven down from Nashville early that morning.

Bishop Finger was our first speaker. He began his remarks by saying, "It surely was a heavy fog covering the roadway as I made my way to here. I could hardly view the road ahead, but I could easily see in the rearview mirror where I had been. That ought to illustrate something." He never did say what that something could or should be. I suppose he thought each person could think for himself. I surmise the real gist of his report was that sometimes the road ahead seems obscure, but to know where we have been helps us to find our way in the future.

For me and, I'm sure, for others, seminary served that purpose quite well. It was a special time for the examination of personal priorities, and there were unselfish, dedicated, and committed people there to help the students to do just that. They were much needed because we were still in a period of transition.

My first thoughts after entering seminary were evil and inaccurate. That is not the best way to begin any endeavor, but maybe a confession is good for my soul.

Some 15 students were seated for an Old Testament class when a professor, Dr. Virgil H. Todd, entered the room. All eyes were on our new teacher, and his eyes were fixed on his new students. I am sure some of the others knew this unusual man, but I had never seen him before. I can still remember the sound of his hard-heeled shoes pounding the hardwood floor as he continued to approach his lectern. A wait-and-see atmosphere embraced this first class session on that early morning. I remember thinking there might not be another man in the city of Memphis who was as mean as this man.

How wrong can a person be? When Dr. Todd reached

126

his lectern, he continued to view his class of seminary freshmen. He called out in a firm, compassionate, charismatic voice, "Good morning, gentlemen." We knew then that we had a teacher who was going to be our friend, as well as a prolific instructor of the subject matter. First impressions do not always tell the full story.

Dr. Todd was filled to the brim with what he taught. His enthusiasm was contagious. From earlier studies, I viewed the Old Testament as dry, factual, and simply historical in nature. But now, the fathers were coming alive. When our new professor raised his voice in excitement and exclaimed, "Now, gentlemen, hear this; this is rich." I knew that heaven and earth were again on friendly terms.

Dr. Todd gave a full measure of his faith and talents. He was not unreasonable in his expectations of his students, but he expected full cooperation from them, as ancient truths became current knowledge. He had little patience with sluggishness of mind and dampness of spirit. He knew that God was not dead and that new revelations were the order of the day. To be taught by such an illuminator was spiritual salve for the sorrowing soul.

This added stability to a life-style that was not always so stable. Many of us had to preach between one and three sermons each weekend, in addition to performing duties at funerals, weddings, church business meetings, pastoral calls, family concerns, and self-interest events.

I had determined that I would attend Jean's school ball games and other youth activities. That resulted in the burning of a lot of late-night oil. There had to be a sharing of time, as well as selves, if personal life was to hold a balance of meaningfulness.

Dr. Todd had help in creating and sustaining a learning environment. The other professors carried their individual loads of community responsibilities. Memphis Theological Seminary maintained a corporate approach to addressing the assorted needs of ministers in the making. No one stood alone, and no one spoke for all of us.

Dr. Irby's careful and meticulous lectures on church history were both interesting and informative. I remember asking him if we needed to comprehend all of the facts and dates when it came time for the examination. He simply replied by telling me, "Yes."

One of the most lingering memories I have of that course was the reminder that, throughout history, many people were neither saints nor sinners but were a combination of both. Yet when it came to the case of Dr. Irby, one could delete the word sinner. He was not only an excellent teacher, but he was a great example of a Christian gentleman.

It has been said that people are known by the company that they keep. To that statement I will add, "The company we keep helps us to see ourselves for who we really are."

Another professor at the seminary was also a most interesting individual. Dr. Aldridge taught some courses in psychology for a time before he moved back to New York. He was a good teacher, but his approach to the subject matter was somewhat unusual. During some of his class lectures and discussions, he would become very personal—relating matters from his personal life. On one occasion, he informed us that he had once had a nervous breakdown. He considered it to be a normal process and believed that after such an illness, a person was stronger than ever.

His therapy was boat racing. He purchased a speedboat and often drove it at maximum speed. He said that it made him feel better. Perhaps that is why Dr. Aldridge dwelt firmly on the question, why do people do as they do?

Reasons for arrogant behavior may include a sense of lost identity, the threat of being ignored, and perhaps an extreme desire to be self-expedient. This product comes in various sizes and colors.

There are times in life when the lights of mental and spiritual illumination are lowered or become a mere glare. This was the situation of a church congregation I was involved with some time before my retirement. A person might think that any group of people living and doing business in a prosperous county seat of West Tennessee would be at peace with themselves, others, and life in general, but this was not the case. It was everything but peaceful. There were various factors that created a negative environment in that situation.

First of all, the former pastor was well educated in subject matter, but his approach to church administration and people involvement was much akin to that of a cult movement. Sometimes, the most useable education comes from sources outside the classroom. Thus, his common sense failed to ripen on the vine. He had been invited to return to the church and aid me in a memorial service. I had never seen the man before that day. He had no reason to have ill feelings about me, but as we waited at the funeral car to lead the procession into the church, he simply kept his back to me and refused to talk. There were those in the church who liked his approach to things, and there were those who hated it.

Second, there was a group of younger adults, parents of school aged and younger children, who were considered outsiders by those who followed the ways of this pastor. Their input in congregational matters was ignored.

Third, there was a group who wanted the members to function as a church, regardless of any differences among members. They seemed to be embarrassed by those who were of a trouble-making nature.

It was alleged that the First United Methodist Church of that city was on the verge of being closed by the conference administration. There seemed to be little hope for reconciliation of the membership.

When I was appointed to that charge, I knew nothing about the situation. I had always had the opinion that a church congregation was capable of administering its own affairs. But this assemblage of people was completely out of control.

It was not long before I was on the receiving end of a negative arrangement of assorted perplexities. My approach to church concerns remained that of doing a minister's work and showing no disrespect for any member. I sought to treat all members in a like manner. I tried to walk a straight line in the middle of a wobbling road.

One person, plus a few others who thought they must dance to her music with no regard for what medley was being played, created the most evident trouble. Two of her followers visited me at the church and the parsonage to discuss the matter. Their position was that I was not the cause of their trouble—it was there before I arrived—but they did not like my treating everyone the same.

My reply was, "My position in this church and every church is to do just what you have indicated. I do not discriminate among people. That is the only way I know to be."

In the early weeks of my residency with that congregation, I was personally approached by the main source of friction. She said, "Either you leave, or I leave, and I don't intend to leave."

I replied, "Well, I am not going anywhere, and I hope you do not either." She soon left, and I remained.

One of those men on the negative side of the aisle did not really want to be there. He appeared to be compelled to resume his faithfulness to his long-standing friend because they had been close associates most of their lives. He was a good man; he just got pulled in the wrong direction, and it was hard for him to break away.

He had a thriving business that covered most of West Tennessee. After he became semifriendly with me, he began to relate how complex it was in his business to keep proper records. "You never know if you are doing everything to satisfy the tax people or not. One can only wonder if the federal government is looking down his back."

Another problem he had was his dislike for lawyers. He didn't trust them with legal matters. I had previously heard him discuss that matter a few times.

Then, on one occasion, he said to me, "Preacher, by the way, you have two brothers who are lawyers, do you not? I know Lyle, who is a Tennessee Supreme Court Justice; who is the other one?"

At this time I was worn nearly threadbare trying to keep the tossing ship from sinking, and I used a bit of strategy that I do not condone. My answer was this: "My other lawyer brother is Frank. He is, and has been for many years, the Federal Court Clerk in Memphis. If you do have problems with the court system, he will choose your jurors." Before this discussion, our friendship was on the mend, but from that time on, it moved into a relationship of mutual respect and appreciation. Also, my position as pastor of that church greatly improved.

Frank never knew that I used him for my own benefit and expediency. But he has always been such a kind, considerate, and thoughtful brother that maybe when he reads this, he will not be too fretful with me. After all, as the saying goes, "Sometimes a man has to do what a man has to do."

I close this briefing with a report I am pleased to give. I remained at that church for five years. I demonstrated no unusual talent in solving the congregation's internal problems, but my willingness to weather the storm, with the help of others, enabled the people to possess a thriving church environment to this day. I have a second to that motion; the minister who followed me later conveyed to one of the earlier dissenters how glad he was to have been appointed to his church. He replied, "If Russell had not been willing to come here and endure the agony he endured, you would not be our pastor now, for there would not be a church here for you to serve."

Sometimes, if the wicks are carefully trimmed and the fuel of faith, desire, and commitment are provided, the small lights of hope can create proper illumination so that people can better see their way as they walk through the streets of life.

PART THREE

Chapter Eleven

Memories

Every story begins somewhere, but beginnings are often difficult to find. The definite origin of a story is as hard to determine as is the narrow line between friendship and love. We may date a story, but we cannot place a limit on its ramifications.

The fact that human life involves so many mysteries is rather baffling but also strangely wonderful. This observation became more real to me in the summer of 1971 while I was vacationing in the mountains of East Tennessee. I found myself contrasting two scenes. One was current; the other was old.

We had paused beside the road to enjoy the beauty and tranquility of our surroundings. It was here that I reflected on the symbolism of a scene involving humanity and nature; four sun-tanned feet were submerged in a crystal clear stream. My daughter, Jean, and Ivan, the young man she was later to marry, were seated side-by-side on a large rock in the middle of the stream. It was only natural for me to wonder what the future would hold for them. But, only time would tell. I realized that this scene and moment would never be repeated. A good story, like life and human experience, moves only in one direction—forward.

My reflections on humanity and nature caused me to remember another significant experience. The scene was a humid, rugged, disease-infested mountainside a few miles outside the city of San Fernando, in the Philippine Islands. The shooting war was over, but the aftermath of human poverty, which always accompanies national or international catastrophes, still was present. My military police company had received orders to search a wilderness area for military deserters, murderers, and people who had committed crimes for which they sought to avoid prosecution. The orders demanded that we remove some blankets from the beds of infant children. In an attempt to relax us all, I repeated to a senior military officer, Staff Sergeant George Clevenger, the title of a familiar song, "Does Your Conscience Ever Bother You?" This effort resulted in some laughter, but it also brought an ache to the heart of at least one soldier, and I am sure that I was not alone in my sadness. As I recall, this was the instant that I first entertained the possibility of dedicating my life to the relief of human suffering.

Such consideration lay dormant for several years, in fact, until a friend, Doc Taylor, startled me by asking, "Have you ever considered preparing for the Christian ministry?" Wishing to put the question out of my mind and completely to rest, I responded in the negative, aware that my response was not entirely truthful.

A few months later, however, I approached the dean of admissions of Lambuth College in Jackson, Tennessee, to discuss my desire to enroll. Many years later, I still remember the expression on Dean Walter H. Whybrew's face as he said, "You have my permission to enroll."

My struggle to survive mentally, emotionally, and financially during these years was further intensified because I was appointed to a ministerial charge one week before I entered college as a full-time student. Financial support was small, and pastoral duties were new and demanding. Parishioners were understanding and supportive, but multitudes of transitions took their toll on my personal happiness. For nearly two years, I fully intended to withdraw from school at some convenient time. My textbooks were new and expensive, but more than once I visualized them flowing down the river that I crossed on my way home each day. Twice, I left the classroom with no intention of ever returning. The first time was near the beginning of the first semester; the second was two weeks later. The first time, my wife persuaded me to return, but the second departure required the joint efforts of her and my sister.

One of my instructors, Dr. James E. Hull, was also very considerate and encouraging. He was truly a friend in time of need, and as I look back, I can see that he had more confidence in me than I had in myself. I returned, graduated, entered seminary the following September, and graduated three years later.

While attending college, I talked with a friend, Reverend W.T. Call, who was familiar with many of the facts surrounding my preparation for the ministry, and he offered this advice: "You should write a book," he said, "and entitle it *I Was a Guinea Pig for the Lord*." I felt that this suggestion was something of a coincidence, as I had previously asked Dr. Hull if I had been admitted in order for them to see if an older person, with as few credentials as I had, could complete the college's requirements for graduation. His quiet and specific answer was, "Yes."

I am not writing these memories because of my

friend's suggestion, nor because of my hardship, but because of my strong conviction that people who try hard enough to succeed may overcome many obstacles that seem to be impossible. I also wish to say that individuals who wrestle successfully with life often find themselves able to enhance the happiness and success of others.

Memories Stimulate

It should not appear strange or unusual that graduations, anniversaries, weddings, and funerals should embrace so much of what is preserved by memory. When one individual tells another about some interesting or unusual event in his life, the incident will so often touch one of these subjects. Intense emotional stimulation propels us into renewed action. Even while writing about things I remember, I am, in a sense, rediscovering degrees of information about myself. I am calling upon myself to remember, to re-evaluate experiences of importance to me and, I hope, others. Some events are easily remembered—they are with us constantly because of personal likes and dislikes; others would also remain and be useful if we were willing to abide by the lessons these memories teach about life.

I used to visit a widower who was in his 80s and still very active and talkative, but his conversations were filled with his memories. He did not talk about what he had done; he talked about what friends he'd had. Several times, he stared at me, his voice beginning to tremble, and tears came to his eyes. "To want to go back to my youthful years would be asking too much. If only I could once again enjoy my 50s, how happy I would be." In essence, he was saying that he had graduated from the things that had meant the most to him."

In this writing, I am intentionally passing over many items that are interesting and amusing to me but that would be of little interest to others. No sensible person should say that all of his experiences have been completely appropriate in every way. They might evoke a degree of humor or interest, but a point substantiated by the silly or sublime serves a negative cause. This is not to say that I have been party to what society might call the major sins, but it is to admit that the human mind and will are not beyond the point of temptation. If this book has any real value, it is not so much in the area of offering a great deal of noble advice on any subject, but it is in the recollection of events with which the reader is compelled to identify. When one reads what another has written, the invitation is before him to consider if it is true of him too. Has this been his story, or could this someday become his interest and involvement?

If something is not remembered as being interesting or rewarding, then there is actually little reason to remember the occasion or event. Some people say we remember what we want to remember and forget what we should forget. But contrary to this theory, common experience reveals that this is not as true as it should be. Many of my experiences that have brought me personal embarrassment and produced negative results have served to remind me that these same mistakes should never be made again.

I strongly believe that the only wedding service in which I did something wrong was one that took place in my home. The bride and groom were both young (though both had been previously married). As far as I knew, there was no legitimate reason that they should not marry again. Many family members had assembled for the event. Near the end of the ceremony, one of the relatives, who was seated immediately behind the standing couple and in front of me, suddenly developed an abundance of enthusiasm for the occasion and expressed herself with an extra amount of smiling. This caught my attention, and instead of pronouncing the couple to be husband and wife, I addressed them as mother and father. I quickly corrected my error in terminology. No one seemed offended by my mistake, but still, I would like very much to have not made this mistake.

Unforgettable memories create impulsive reactions when subjected to renewed recognition. Television talk shows and soap operas enjoy an abundance of viewers, not because they expect to receive any outstanding information on the various subjects discussed, but because an abundant display of public social interaction provides the interested person with a large range of subject matter with which he may identify. Informative reviews and discussions of so many things on these programs provide the opportunity for one to rediscover himself and his interests, calling his entire value system into current action.

Cards, keepsakes, and preserved trinkets also serve to help us remember lessons that we should not forget. On one occasion, I was conducting a memorial service where several of the family members present were deaf. Arrangements were made to have a professional interpreter on hand. When I rose to speak, she stood facing me and began to recite with her hands and fingers in symbolic language the exact words and statements I was speaking. All went well until I became fascinated by the interpreter's smooth rhythm of gestures. When I momentarily became more interested in what she was doing than in what I was saying, her hands suddenly broke their systematic pace. This reminded me that when broken statements or useless

words are extended, the result is not one of positive significance. I learned an important lesson on that occasion:
Extract from your daily experiences that which is eter-
nally lasting and helpful, and forget the rest. Preserve experiences of quality, and destroy those that have no
lasting value. This helps to strengthen the type, quality,
and character of reflection that presents itself for future
reference.

Refreshed By Recreation

If life did not have a way of embracing us with a variety of experiences, no sensitive person could long hold
onto his sanity. Even when hurt and harm become the
companions of one's daily events, periodic relief is made
possible by the transition of changing circumstances. No
one is ever completely free of tensions and regressions,
but lucky is the individual who compels even the adversities to render him a little richer understanding of life.
Nevertheless, unusual things have a way of surfacing in
the most inconspicuous places.

I began to attend high school football games for no
better reason than that some of the young men in my
church were playing on the local team. I thought their
pastor should show some interest in their recreational activities. As time went on, this became less of a chore. My
family and I began to enjoy all of the amusement associated with this good sport. Furthermore, this was during
my senior year in college, and it was a relaxing break from
the constant strain of travel and study.

The school had an excellent team that year and went
on to win the championship for the district. My ministerial
appointment was suddenly changed, but fortunately, it
was not so far away that I could not return for that out-

standing event of the season. That night became a most memorable occasion for some of us, in more ways than one. The game was so well attended that we had to enter the stadium an hour early in order to get a seat. Even then, people were crowded around both the end zones, and many had nowhere to sit. Christine and I went with her brother and his wife. We happened to make our way into the bleachers at an area where there was just enough space for four people to sit. Our seating arrangement became more interesting when we realized that some of our friends happened to be seated in front of us. One of them—a very jolly and talkative young lady—had often teased me that I reminded her of her father, even though I was only a few years older than she was.

Christine started to sit on the outside next to a beautiful young lady, but then she said for me to sit there. She reminded me that I usually ended up in the middle where the cold wind could not touch me. "OK, that's all right with me," was my reply. Our friend in front of us introduced us to her cousin, Regina Stacks, who appeared to be in her middle 20s and was wearing an engagement ring large enough to be easily noticed. It was such a cold night that blankets and spreads almost covered the entire stadium. Christine and I were enjoying the snug comfort of our G. I. blanket and were engaged in conversations with those about us when I happened to notice that my new friend was unescorted and was actually shivering from the cold weather and had no extra wrap for comfort. I estimated the distance across our four laps and discovered that there was enough blanket to cover the lap of one additional person.

I felt a little odd for making such an offer to a stranger, but I pushed aside my reservations and inquired, "Would you like to share our wrap with us?"

Memories

"I surely would," was her reply.

The game started, and a better ball game I had never seen—one team led, then the other. Enthusiasm and cheers ran high. Spectators found themselves unable to remain seated. There was nearly as much standing as there was sitting. Conversation was not lacking on the warm side, which Christine had chosen, so I felt it was socially appropriate for me to do a little conversing with my new friend, who had been compelled to share our space with us. Actually, she was difficult to ignore because she became so involved in the game that jars and jabs became the order of the evening. This was nothing unusual. I was frequently jarred around in friendly scuffles with my teenage daughter, but when excitement reached the point that long, well-manicured fingernails began to penetrate the sleeve of my coat, I thought, I don't know how long I can take this. It would have appeared rude to remind Miss Stacks to be more restrained, and I decided to bear the burden without crying out for help.

All was moving forward in the name of clean fun and wholesome entertainment, and I felt there was no reason for alarm. That is, everything was fine until I happened to look down toward the other end and discovered that my sister-in-law had been stripped of her portion of our community property. The blanket had been so gradually moved to the left that every one had begun to notice this except me. There had never been any reason for tension between Christine and me over improper social behavior, but when I observed this situation, I thought, *Boy, there is going to be trouble at my house tonight.* My second thought was, *Old boy, you have been a good and proper sport up to this point, and there is no reason to blow it now.* I did, however, begin an inch by inch ordeal of easing that blanket back to its original position.

The game ended, and I received a most sincere expression of appreciation for my hospitality. We all began to leave. I still thought that I was in for a nice lecture because of my generosity to this nice person, but not a word was forthcoming. I have always appreciated the fact that my wife was a better sport than I had anticipated. It was quite a game, quite an experience, quite an unforgettable evening. Such recreation was not only refreshing to me but it also helped me to be more appreciative of others.

Chapter Twelve

Friendship

The Rewards of Friendship

There are rewards in life for those who can remember that which should be remembered and forget that which should be forgotten. Memory provides the substance out of which past experience is examined for future use. My own ability to remember depends largely upon events that are either shocking or especially pleasing. A variety of both have characterized my life for many years.

I remember well a lady I met only once. That was an unforgettable experience because she wrapped me in a fine fur coat on a cold, lonely night. But more than that, she wrapped me in her heart because her own son would never know her love again. These words are offered in the form of an imaginary letter:

Dear Mrs. Doctor:
You probably won't remember me, but I remember you. The reason for this is very simple. I am the one who happened to be the recipient of your unusual and unmerited grace. All I gave to you was a reminder of what you once had, but held no longer. There is no reason for my telling you that you had

just lost a son, a soldier, in the European theater of war in the early months of 1945. You said his age was the same as mine. As we rode together on that speeding and unusually cold passenger train from Chattanooga to Memphis, Tennessee, you related this information to me. I had just told you that most of the young soldiers aboard with us, including myself, were en route to join other Pacific forces for the invasion of Japan. I remember so well your intense observation of me. It was my conviction that you were wondering if I, too, would have to die so young. When we said good-bye, I couldn't say it too well. Please forgive me. You were about 40 years of age at that time, a very lovely lady, and the wife of a Memphis physician.

I was a little embarrassed the next morning when I awoke from my reclining seat, all neatly attired in your beautiful black fur coat. You had ridden cold, and I knew why. You had placed upon me a token of affection that you would have joyfully given to your son. No earthly honor can excel such a tribute as that. Now, 33 years later, I still count this as one of the greatest honors and memories of my life. You were not bitter over your tragic loss, but I'm sure there was an ache in your heart that time has never quite erased. My sense of regret is that, during all of these years, I did not make the necessary effort to meet you again, learn your name, and tell you, as best I could, what an impact your kindness has had on my life. But our daily lives and efforts of living have a way of keeping us busy—too busy—until, often, it's too late to make proper amends.

144

I trust that life has been good to you and that your rich contributions to the cause and efforts to establish a degree of "peace on earth and good will among men" have given you a sense of pride—the likes of which shall forever live in the annals of righteous history. Perhaps you will agree with me when I say the greatest testimonies are never written or recorded; they are felt most of all in positive results for human betterment. The world may soon forget our unselfish deeds, but let it always be remembered that the purest crowns are worn in the unselfish hearts of those who gave until it actually hurt. There are those who know best of all the unselfish spirit behind such benevolent devotion.

There is a further thought I would invite you to join me in remembering. These are my words, and I would like to leave them with you: Genuine love knows no special time or distance; raptured emotion cleaves best of all to memory; human compassion struggles for expression, even when cultured by adversity.

To such a friend for such a short duration, I wish to say, You lost a son so early in both of your lives, but you made a friend who has remembered you all of these years. Thank you for the warmth of your garment, but thank you most of all for sharing with a stranger a degree of human compassion, even when troubled yourself. Your kindness has helped to keep alive a most cherished and sacred memory of a very special person. When I think of the past, I often think of your precious memory and offer a silent prayer of gratitude for your short and unusual friendship.

The Cultivation of Friendship

This chapter is dedicated to my friends: people who have befriended me in time of mutual pleasures, as well as in times of negative circumstance and acute loneliness. These individuals sought to see some positive characteristic in me even when little effort was demonstrated on my part to do the same. Such kindness reminds me of not only my indebtedness to others but also that friendship is something freely given that should never be taken for granted. Instead, it should be cultivated with extreme care.

The friendship of some college students and faculty members once helped to ease my pain. I had received a D- for a college course when it was evident that I had earned a B. A professor had become upset with me because I would not spy on my fellow classmates in an attempt to discover who had stolen a final examination paper. This immature behavior was made even worse by the instructor's insinuation that I might have been the guilty party. Others knew this was not true and urged me to dismiss the misery from my mind.

There was another time when friendship aided my composure. A small group in my church became dissatisfied with my role as their pastor because I continued to advocate a church administration policy of all-share-and-share-alike instead of the type of situation where a few set the policy and proceedings for all of the members. This group found a friend in one member of the pastoral committee who reported to an official meeting, "The pastor is lazy, wears dirty clothes, is uneducated, can't preach acceptable sermons, and does not know the members of the congregation." I was present when this report was given and labeled it Five Assumptions Provided by Proxy.

Friendship

I shall always appreciate the fine support and Christian spirit of nearly all of the people in that Chester church, but one friend, Mrs. Patsy Henderson, made a statement that helped me very much. In her quiet and genuine manner, she said, "Don't allow trite opinions to cause you to become caught up in insignificant matters."

Friendship is expressed in many ways. But the friendships that are the most apt to endure are those that are cultivated by mutual respect and joyful participation in matters of mutual interest.

On one occasion, I was among a group of 17 men who were at an overnight camp in Natchez Trace State Park. We were anxious to enter the forest the next morning before daylight and search for deer. In the meantime, we entertained ourselves with delicious food and humorous conversation.

One talkative fellow in the group, Paul Stimpson, contributed one of the last stories before we retired that night. His story was that he had purchased a $1,500 coonhound the year before and the dog was worth every cent of the purchase price. "This dog has become so good that I no longer have to go hunting with him in order to catch raccoons. All I have to do is place the size of board by the gate to show him what size of coonskin would be needed for a particular stretching." Then, the owner paused and said very seriously, "But, you know, I'm worried. My dog hasn't been home in three weeks. I'm afraid he is lost."

Here, I thought perhaps I might be able to cheer his master up a bit. "Are you sure your wife didn't accidentally place the ironing board outside the door of your house while rearranging the furniture? He's probably just still looking."

He stared and replied, "How did you know that?"

147

My personal nature does not lend itself to the idling away of a great deal of time or energy. For this reason, it is quite hard for some people to understand how I can sit in a deer stand for five hours at a time, waiting for a chance to take a shot at an evasive animal. The nonsportsman may not be aware there is a solitude in the confines of nature that is very scarce in other places. One has time to think, to ponder the past, and to become excited about the future. Such an environment lends itself to the destruction of matters of minor importance. It allows one to breathe freshness into his character and exhale mental and social rubbish that pollutes his life. I'm not alone in practicing the pleasures of outdoor sportsmanship or knowing that good experiences become better when they are shared.

Not everyone will allow another to practice on his patience or experiment with his sense of humor. I met Dr. Bill McColgan and his medical staff when I was in acute need of dental surgery. Bill's father-in-law specialized in this type of practice, and I met him first. After he had completed my treatment, he reminded me that I needed to see someone else for further professional care. Dr. Marcus Jones suggested that I might like to see his son-in-law, Dr. Bill.

After the second appointment, the doctor and I entered the hallway. A repairman wearing a belt filled with tools entered the walkway just in front of us. I suddenly developed an impulse to check my new friend's sense of humor by announcing to him, "I am glad I drew you instead of him." His comfortable laughter presented me with extra pleasure for having come to know and share a few moments of delightful social exchange with someone previously unknown to me.

This sort of introduction was to lead later to the planning and execution of a hunting trip for us. We agreed to have breakfast at my home and then drive some 40 miles to my brother-in-law's farm, which was well populated with deer. Breakfast was rushed. I cooked the ham too fast, and it was a little tough, but that didn't seem to hinder our early morning appetites. Then we hit the road, filled with great expectations of bringing home some fresh venison, as well as a trophy head.

We arrived at our destination at an appropriate hour. It was still dark. We took our lights and walked through a forest, then through a bean field to a very choice and comfortable stand, from which I had previously taken three bucks. This stand was built for this purpose. I had constructed a reclining chair—angle iron welded together and a rope-plaited cushioned seat. It was stationary against a large white-oak tree and was approximately 12 feet above the ground, with some good limbs on each side for additional comfort.

I expected that my friend would take a nice buck as soon as it became daylight. In fact, one was already nearby. We heard him take a few leaps to clear our path as we were coming in. I assumed this old fellow didn't stampede and leave, because a few minutes later, when I came out of the field, he was still there. This was an area the deer used frequently; there were many tracks, scrapes, and rubs in the immediate vicinity.

I suppose it is true with most people who go into the fields to hunt that the most interesting things that happen are those that happen to one's associates, especially the humorous things. This trip was odd. After my companion took his place in my stand, I moved on down the field to a place I had chosen for myself. When I paused to load my weapon and settle down for a quiet wait, I discovered that my ammunition was missing. Some time later it was found at this very spot; however, there in the darkness, my cartridges were not to be found. I reasoned that I must have left them in my truck. I was returning on the opposite side of the field from Dr. Bill, but his curiosity became too much for him. "Where are you going? What's wrong?" He inquired from a distance. This curious predicament was explained as quietly as possible, and I moved on through the forest. But, to my dismay, my needed supplies were not there. I decided to return to the lone, still hunter in the stand and tell him that I would take a nap in the truck and wait for him. I knew fully well that moving about had destroyed any chance of us seeing a deer that morning. But, my associate invited me to join him in his perch in the white oak. "Come on and get up with me. I have some coffee. We'll talk awhile."

I began to consider this suggestion as being odd, coming from a seasoned sportsman. Doesn't he know that talking while doing this type of hunting is not appropriate? However, I did join my good-natured friend in the tree-house type seat. The coffee was delicious, and we did talk, especially when it was mentioned how unusual this would appear should another hunter come by and discover our arrangement.

A difficult explanation was to come later. The doctor's aid wanted to know if we had had any luck. It seemed he had told her just enough about what happened to arouse her intense curiosity. A few days later when I returned for another visit, some questions were quickly forthcoming. Mary's look of amazement was more questioning than were her questions. She quietly admitted that this all seemed so strange. "Never before have I heard such a story. When you come to think of it, a doctor and a preacher having a tea-party in the same tree when they are supposed to be hunting is hard to believe. That taxes my imagination, much less my sense of humor." A rational explanation is not always needed in order to appreciate something that happens. The part of the story we remember and talk about most is the humor we extracted from the trip. Sharing these events of mutual interest helped to establish a friendship that I cherish very much.

An Imposition on Friendship

Individuals are capable of experiencing great joy but may also be the bearers of intense sorrow. The daily sentiments of almost everyone may be reflected in these words: Our daily experiences are little more than the fluctuation of feelings—all the way from elation to drudgery. Composure depends upon mental, moral, and spiritual posture being developed by well-disciplined norms, minds, and faiths.

While John Dunivant and I were attending seminary at the Memphis Theological Seminary, we relaxed together on our trips that were often characterized by humorous conversation. This was important for both of us because school, ministerial responsibilities, and family concerns all combined to create very tight schedules. I am certain that these types of involvement were what caused John to seek some mental relief in a Greek class shortly before he graduated.

Greek was not one of his most enjoyable subjects because Dr. Caldwell's practice was for students to translate one Bible sentence at a time into the historical language. On one occasion, my friend looked ahead to determine which line he would get but made a wrong choice. The professor became a little impatient with his student's academic progress at this point. When tension began to mount, John rose to his feet and said, "Dr. Caldwell, surely heaven will be worth it all," and sat down.

Perhaps a variety of personal concerns explained our readiness to impose a bit on the friendship of Fred King, who at the time was doing his work for a master's degree at Memphis State University. Fred lived in Memphis during the week and would return with us to his home, near Ripley, each Friday evening. Fred and I had attended college together. It was common knowledge that he was a brilliant student. To be honest, I think John and I secretly envied his scholastic abilities. He didn't have to work as hard to get good grades as we did. This helped to explain our eagerness to badger our friend with offers for free clerical officiating at any service of marriage that he might arrange during the ensuing Thanksgiving holidays. John and I were aware that Fred had never shown noticeable interest in this type of relationship. He was quite able to defend himself, and this he promptly did.

But these humorous and even ridiculous discussions lasted for only a short time. About 15 miles outside of the city on Highway 14, we suddenly became party to a tragedy that immediately transformed all foolishness into extreme sorrow and compassion for all who had been involved in a disastrous automobile wreck.

A county school bus driver had been engaged in discharging grade-school children near their homes along the heavily traveled highway. We were the first to arrive on the scene and quickly discovered, beside the bus, in front of a car, the body of a little girl who had been hit as she attempted to cross the intersection. A man who appeared to be in his early 70s was the driver of the car that struck the child. He and his wife gave evidence of being very near a state of shock. Our traveling associate informed John and me that this wreck was none of his business and remained in the car, leaving the two of us to console the bereaved, direct the traffic, and answer questions from anxious motorists as they steered slowly past the blanketed body of the deceased. The state police arrived after an hour, relieving two mentally worn-out ministers of the bearing of these various burdens.

Hopefully, we learn something from all persons, places, and events. Two lasting memories often refresh the personal pain of that event: One, the often-repeated question asked by motorists as they were directed on their way, "Is the child black or white?"

After several such inquiries, I answered, "It is a child." Second, the most intense expression of grief I have ever witnessed was visible on the face of the child's mother when she arrived on the scene and raised the blanket from the body of her little girl. Possibly, the few minutes of humorous conversation enjoyed by two of us and endured by another immediately prior to the event helped prepare us to be kind to those who were in desperate need along the highway that cold November day some years ago.

Chapter Thirteen

Embarrassment

History continues to record one unusual discovery after another. Science and mythology continue to reveal both facts and fiction that aid the telling of the human story. Each era of civilization continues its own deposits of unusualness, but the human race has never departed very far from its original stance in the overall scheme of creation. Always at its side is the fact that the first people did not hold seniority over all matter and motion. Since the beginning of time, both animals and humans have been compelled to either adjust to each other or perish. The law of the jungle—the survival of the fittest—still affects length of life and circumstance of death.

I find an interesting moral in this observation. Unless persons learn by trial and error, they soon become wards of the state or little more than statistics. "It matters little from whence cometh the wisdom. The important thing is to get wisdom, and in the getting of wisdom, get understanding" (Proverbs 4:5). This lesson was momentarily forgotten at the Hungry Bear Restaurant in Murray, Kentucky, a few years ago when three companions and I stopped there for lunch en route home from a ministerial retreat in another part of that state.

I had never been there before and was not aware that a very large bear was mounted on a coil spring at the side of the front entrance to the dining room. A conversation was in progress as we passed single-file through the door. The person in front of me bumped the bear and sent it into a backward tilt. As I reached the animal, it was time for the huge form to move forward. His claws caught me in the arm with a great deal of force. Without looking, I thought that someone was being rude, but when I turned sideways and observed the wide-mouthed monster quickly moving in on me, I almost cleared the building in one great stride. My friends still tease me about arguing with that most unusual animal.

That was not my last encounter with inhuman forms of creation in public places. Sometime later, I found myself unable to demonstrate any superiority over my animal associates. I had decided that a herd of goats would not only be a profitable investment but would also help prevent disease in my small herd of cattle.

After making some inquiries, I discovered where I could purchase four of these cute, but cunning creatures. True to my custom of identifying by individual names every animal on the farm, I gave each goat a name: Nannie, Hannie, Bannie, and Blackboy. The three females were very white and almost identical in appearance, but the male goat fit his descriptive title quite well.

In order to take them to the farm, I had to go through Jackson, a fairly large city. A short time before this, I had purchased a new pickup truck. Not wanting to scratch it by using sideboards, I obtained some lumber and made a slatted shipping crate that fit quite well into the bed of the truck. I put my goats into the crate, and all went well until I began to pass down the last long street of the city. Only

Blackboy spoke as we became city travelers. Trying not to disturb my passengers, I braked the truck gently to a stop at the first traffic signal. The only person waiting to cross the intersection was an overweight woman. The silence was broken by Blackboy's loud and clear bleat—a very strong mating call. Since the goats were out of sight and I was the only visible traveler, there was only one apparent source for this rude and unnecessary greeting—the driver of the truck, yours truly. This circuit rider became the recipient of a harsh stare and what is sometimes referred to as a royal cussing. That woman criticized my ancestors something awful. My first thought was to apologize for Blackboy's ill manners, but who would have believed that a goat was being hauled in that truck? My second thought was to just pay no attention to the woman. The light changed, and I quickly drove away.

One shock in a day is not always enough. I was fast approaching another traffic light, almost praying that this scene would not be repeated. But, the light was changing to red. Sure enough, there stood another lone woman waiting to cross to the other side of the street. My over-anxious stock again became very sensitive to his current environment—the humidity of an August day and the odors of the city—and made a personal announcement of his presence. As compared to the first call, the second one only served as a prelude to shock my trembling senses. Blackboy really spoke as though he possessed all of the necessary masculinity for living in the wild. Again, I was shocked, but joyfully so. This pedestrian simply gave me a nice, and seemingly understanding smile and went on her way.

It is wonderful that all people are not alike. It is great that some individuals are willing to be tolerant and to display understanding when they are exposed to aggravation. Surely, wisdom must be embraced by understanding in order to cultivate its virtue. Undisciplined wisdom is a serious threat to society, but when the element of compassion is added, happiness is the end result. I remember the person who called me some ugly names, but I remember most of all, the nice lady who demonstrated a full measure of compassion for a stressful traveler.

Confused, But Interested

Some of my friends have told me that I have more experiences than most people have. I don't think this is necessarily true. I believe that one has to help formulate a few eventful experiences from time to time, but everything is not the seed of fate or fortune. One must make a few deposits into the checking account of experience in order to draw something out. Everyone, if he chose to carefully observe his assorted experiences, could produce some interesting stories. Probably, the reason many people fail to do so is that everyone is not willing to run the risk of placing his thoughts and actions on display for public consideration. For example, I once fixed the wrong tire for a stranger I met on the road. When some of the details of this event were learned by Charley Morgan, he said to me, "I would never have told that."

Certainly, I can keep secrets; I would never betray the trust and confidence that others have placed in me. But, something as humorous as failing to distinguish between a good car tire and a tire that had blown out, borders on the side of the hilarious and should be shared.

On a humid day, I was returning from a funeral service. I had been following another car for only a short distance when a front tire blew out and almost came off of the wheel. The driver steered the wobbling vehicle to the shoulder of the road. My first thought was that I was not too good to do a little missionary work on the side of the road. The young woman, who was a stranger to me, was a bit upset with her husband. She said, "He drove the good car today and left this trap for me to use." As I listened to her talk about her misfortune of the hour, I proceeded with the task of getting the stranded traveler mobile again. I opened the trunk of her car, retrieved the bumper jack, and placed it at the back of the car. The front tire, though, was the one that was flat.

The lady did not notice the difference, and neither did I until the lugs had been removed, and I had placed my hands on each side of a firm tire to remove the wheel. The instant that my fingers grasped the wheel, I knew I had made a big mistake. What made this situation so humorous to me was that I had recently completed the construction of a homemade vehicle. That machine worked perfectly, but here I was working on the wrong tire. My mistake was not mentioned. I continued to turn the lugs in the proper direction. Traffic was heavy, and so was my intense desire to laugh. The old folk song "All Shook Up" would have very aptly described this confusion.

My hands were still holding the wrench when a car stopped nearby. "There goes Uncle John," said the constantly speaking woman. As it turned out, Uncle John was also an effective spokesman. "You have two flats" was his first remark when he approached our proximity. "This one on the front is also down."

My reply was, "Yes, I know that, but I'm working my way in that direction." He was offered the job, and I went on my way.

For some time, I felt assured that this mistake was new

in the annals of highway experiences. But, some two years later, a banker from Nashville, Tennessee, was speaking at the local industrial banquet and related an almost identical situation, which happened to a friend of his. I could hardly wait for him to finish his speech, so I could speak to someone who knew that this type of thing could actually happen.

I have read that the ability to laugh at oneself is a sign of greatness. If this is true, I may have more in my favor than I sometimes believe. A series of revival services was being held at a church where a friend of mine was pastor. I was speaking on this particular occasion. My minister-friend had previously told the congregation enough of the above story to arouse the curiosity of some members, causing them to wonder what type of individual had been invited to speak in their church. Several began to ask me more details of the event. One night I took time, at the beginning of the service, to relate the story in almost its entirety. I don't think I have ever heard more laughter, especially in church. Even after thoughts should have been moving in more serious channels, one man suddenly gave out a renewed yell, "Oh, ho, ho." This caused me to almost lose control of myself for the entire hour.

What I found to be the most amusing happened after the service had been completed while many people were standing outside the building talking in the semidarkness. One man eased up to me and inquired very quietly, "Now, preacher, why did you really take off the wrong tire?"

I smiled and replied, "That's the part I never have told." We had a good revival, and no harm seemed to have been done to the sentiments and religious composure of those who attended the services.

It is my conviction that redemption of an individual's mind and will is necessary before the human heart can undergo Christian transformation. If all personal experience were designed for moral perfection, then there would be less need for any reflections of casual concerns.

When I was in school, I became aware of the fact that much of our subject matter catered to the negative issues of Christian faith and daily living. I learned to discriminate—to compare statements and facts with my moral values. The prophet Isaiah spoke of the human situation when he said, "Woe is me, for I am undone; I am a man of unclean lips" (Isaiah 6:5).

There is a vast difference between vulgarity and good clean humor. Humor may well serve as the means of identifying personal needs and shortcomings. Whatever is used, when morally right, to aid our maturing Christian character is a blessing that should not be denied to anyone.

Mental and spiritual sluggishness brought on by overworked and overtaxed bodies has a way of creating slow responses to values of a supreme nature. An intense spiritual posture has to be cultivated and used to aid good maturation to receive the blessing of the Lord. He, too, often appealed to the casual enjoyment of his subjects before going on to tell the big story, which was often introduced by a smaller story of human interest. An individual is, first and always, a person. One never departs from such a status. It behooves us to be aware of the many areas and compartments of human nature that desire fulfillment.

For a short time, I became fearful that the current administrator and spiritual leader of our conference had forgotten this. Some of us who were recent seminary graduates had been graciously invited to his home for a dinner in honor of our graduation. Christine caused a sudden and startled expression on his face when she began a casual conversation by saying, "Bishop, I'm not sure I approve of the idea of our husbands being sent to other areas of the state on exchange preaching missions. The week after Russell returned from such a trip, he received a letter from the motel maid." Our host's first reply was a long, drawn-out, "Yes." I suddenly felt that the "U-Haul Express" was about to roll again. I further believed it had become my time to speak, and speak I did.

I explained that when preparing to leave the motel, I picked up some postal cards, which I had not used during the week, and wrote a note of appreciation to the one who had kept my apartment so clean, neat, and livable during my stay away from home. I believe that race, creed, social status, conference relationship, geographical location, or any other factor should not prevent one from being kind to another. The tone of the conversation took on a more acceptable manner when the custodian's words were repeated. "I have worked here for six years. This is the first time during all of that time that anyone ever bothered to thank me for my services to them during their stay in this motel." It was a beautiful letter. It remains one of my most cherished keepsakes. I don't know the extent of any good that my sermons produced in the church that week, but I am most certain that the one written on that postal card has been remembered and appreciated until this very day.

Ministerial Calls

Not only does a minister quite frequently serve as a friend to the faithful but he also serves, at times, as a shock absorber for the timid, the rude, and the mean. Thus, he is prone to feel, from time to time, that he is being sacrificed for the public good.

As a child who grew up in a family of churchgoing

people, I thought everyone was always anxious to have his minister call at his home. I have since changed my mind. I frequently find myself competing with a television program, an evening nap, and, sometimes, the daily nip. In the vast majority of cases, the pastor, if he calls at an appropriate hour, is accepted graciously and is made to feel that he is actually someone of importance to the entire family. But wise, indeed, is the visitor who is aware that circumstances can change from door to door.

The Clark family had recently moved to my pastoral charge when I visited the family. George Clark greeted me with all of the friendliness and courtesy that anyone should expect. He offered to serve me a cocktail. When I declined, he said, "Well, will you have a beer with me?" I was offering another polite refusal when his wife entered the living room and began to explain to her husband that social customs in our section of the country were somewhat different from those in the area where they had lived. My great concern was how to decline the offer of my gracious host without offending him. His wife was very helpful at this point.

These radical differences are not always confined to human activities. One spring day, I went to call on another family who had recently moved into the community. As I parked my car at the gate, I noticed the family car was parked nearby and made my way toward the front entrance of the house. I suddenly met with the most vicious, black shepherd dog I had ever encountered. It was too late to return to my car, and as it happened, there was no one at home to rescue me from this gun-powder-fed beast. He wrapped his front legs around the mid-section of my body and spread his mouth over my left side. I did not especially mind that he was damaging my clean suit with his saliva, but I was very concerned about his teeth pressing in quite hard over a vital organ of my body, as deep gurgling snarls issued from his vicious throat.

I quickly considered the situation and decided there were only two alternatives and that neither of them offered me any comfort. I might be able to get off one hard stroke with my foot to the underside of this outraged animal. But, would that allow me to follow through with an additional protective maneuver? I dismissed that idea with my conviction that one small flinch would be all of the incentive that was needed to motivate the dog to take out a sizeable slice of my trembling body. Thus, I attempted the second alternative: I tried to talk him out of attacking me. Not once did this ill-tempered animal get back to the ground on all four feet before we reached my car; he continued to embrace me with his front legs as though he had suddenly found a new and interesting dance partner. At frequent intervals, I could feel the tightening squeeze of his legs as he gave out one evil snarl after another. I attempted to use some verbal persuasion as we stepped slowly and carefully backward. "Come on, old boy. Come on and don't be excited. Everything will be all right. I did not mean any harm by coming into your yard. Come on and be a nice boy." I used this strategy until I was able to vacate his territory. This humoring conversation worked. As I eased the car door open and easily dropped into the seat, it seemed to dawn on the beast that the intruder was actually going to go free. He then plunged into the outside of the passenger door. My sturdy little Renault became worth every cent of its purchase price. Now that I was shielded from danger, it was truly a haven of rest in the midst of a raging storm. Before leaving, or while getting in shape to leave, I remember quite well re-

minding myself that even the dogs are not resisting and
hampering my ministerial efforts.

There was another time when my personal powers of
vocal persuasion were not as effective. The results of this
event helped to create a unique friendship that has lasted
until this very day. But the first few minutes of this
Monday visit caused some doubt that such would be the
case. During an informal discussion, following my first service at a new appointment, Mr. Sanford Grimes told me
how to locate his home. In fact, I remembered my having
seen it on the way to church that morning. The following
day, I was anxious to let the parishioners know that I was
on the job, so I visited the Grimes. After the usual greetings, I inquired, "Where is your father? Does he come
home for lunch?" Immediately, I realized I had made an
error in judgment. The person I was talking to was his
wife, not his daughter.

Her nearly hysterical laughter was truly soothing to
my mental sores. I really appreciated the lovely manner in
which she accepted my mistake. At that instant, the door
opened and Mrs. Grimes called out, "Here comes Daddy
now." No doubt, that was the happiest ending to what
began as the most confused pastoral call that I ever made.

Developing An Appreciation For Humor

Humor can offset many negative situations. Struggling
with the combined demands of college and the pastoral
duties of three churches, I soon realized that my mind and
spirit had to find ways for renewal and refreshment.
Otherwise, I would remain captivated by fear, frustration,
and regression. Cultivating a better appreciation for
humor helped a great deal. William Barclay has written,
"Perseverance plus cheerfulness will get a man almost

anywhere. Even if they don't get him all of the way, they will make him laugh wherever he arrives. The world needs people like that."[19]

I first began to develop a sense of humor when a large group from my hometown gathered near Jackson, Mississippi, for a wedding rehearsal at the church of the bride-to-be. The drive was long; the day was humid. The church was nearly filled for the rehearsal. I was to officiate at the wedding, but interesting events were not to wait that long.

The wedding participants were in place. A young lady, Miss Jo Anne Simmons, who was a college soprano, and Mrs. Thomas Akin, a pianist, were seated at my side in a front corner of the sanctuary, waiting to rehearse the ceremony. I crossed my knees and moved slightly forward across the pew. I thought I heard my trousers rip. I placed my left hand on my hip and discovered my pants had been altered by the tiny tip of a protruding tack. Quickly, I turned to Jo Anne and announced, "I have torn my trousers."

She exclaimed in disbelief, "Oh, no!"

I reassured her in the same tone of voice, "Oh, yes!"

It was time for me to take my place at the center of the altar. The stand-ins for the bride and groom were about to come forward. As I passed by the musicians, who were still seated in the corner of the church, their strained, muffled grunts were clearly audible. My thought at the time was, I know you are having some fun at my expense, but not nearly so much as you would have had if I had not given you a short verbal preview of what was to come. I have long had the opinion that when the element of surprise is removed, much of the excitement is also destroyed. I didn't mind providing these people with a little joy, but I assumed it would be more appropriate to reserve uncontrolled laughter for another occasion.

Nothing yet had produced as much tension and as many thought-provoking expressions as did the noticeable consternation visible on the face of my wife as she sat beside an older lady near the rear of the building. Her interest in current events seemed to increase as I walked to the center of the altar and slid my arms out of my coat, allowing the garment to ease down my back until it covered the point of current widespread interest. With an astonished expression, mingled with panic and disbelief at what her eyes were seeing, she moved to a light perch on the edge of the pew. I'm sure such a performance, even in this old church building, must have been reserved for that very hour.

That evening, after the rehearsal, the groom dove into the swimming pool and broke his nose. He later told me that his greatest fear at the time was that the bride might forget that they were not Eskimos and want to rub noses instead of using the traditional kiss after the benediction was pronounced concluding the ceremony.

Mental and social adjustments are not always easily made. Yet, a positive approach to the unexpected can turn embarrassment into wholesome experience. The humor extracted from these accidents more than compensated for our anxiety.

No Escape From Involvement

I feel sure that shocking events have occurred in every profession. There is no place to hide from public involvement for those who offer a service that is of a social nature. The Christian ministry is no exception. There is another interesting fact associated with ministering to people; the best way to get to really know people is to observe their conduct during stressful experiences.

A few years ago, a 90-year-old man and his younger wife moved from Memphis to a rural community near Ripley, Tennessee. This couple attended the worship services at my church twice before the husband's death. Late one evening, I was notified that I would be expected to hold the memorial service for this man, who was reputed to be the nephew of President Abraham Lincoln's wife. As my wife and I entered the funeral parlor and approached his casket, we were met by the wife of the deceased. For a few seconds, in silence, we stood beside the body of her late husband. The silence was broken when Mrs. Todd remarked, "Well, I did the best I could for him while he was living. I'm looking for another man now."

I was rather anxious to get outside so I could have those remarks verified. That was no problem because my companion was just as anxious as I was to comment on the bereaved wife's having made plans this early in her state of widowhood.

This type of attitude did help to ease my responsibilities for counseling at that time, but it also reminded me that there are times when one should remain silent after another speaks, including showing respect for one's departed spouse. I was somewhat speechless at this point. This unusual experience followed no previous example, and it took a little time for me to make proper adjustments. The wife's remark was not immoral or repulsive, just different.

No Time For Foolishness

A wedding was scheduled at my former church in Ripley. I was invited to officiate at the service. The rehearsal was held the evening before. The necessary plans and precautions were taken to ensure that the ceremony would complement the occasion. During the rehearsal, I advised the wedding director that I did not know the classical music being used for the wedding march and would need some specific help to enter the sanctuary at the proper time. This obstacle further complicated the situation; I had an intense roaring in my ear. She replied, "Don't worry. Leave the door slightly ajar, and I will motion to you at the proper moment." This was done.

The entire wedding party was in its place before the altar. Persons of special honor were seated, and she gave me the signal to enter. I was followed by the groom and the best man. While walking these few steps, I thought that we were doing this just as it should be done. But my sense of well-doing was doomed to short duration. The organist kept on playing some prearranged music, which she could have easily cut short and changed to the wedding march. Instead, she called out to me, "You are not supposed to be in here." So, in front of a completely filled church, we turned and marched out with all of the dignity we had used to enter. I had always thought I would faint if this ever happened to me, but I didn't.

Once again, the wedding director nodded to me, and, again, we made the approach to the altar. On this return trip, I heard the voice of the groom, behind me, saying in a low, soft tone, "Wrong song."

I responded, "We stay this time."

A local attorney and friend of the family, Lewis Walker, called out to me from across the street the next day. "It was a beautiful wedding—once they decided to let you marry them." The director was intensely hurt and apologized very kindly for this mistake. Yet, I was not about to punish her even more by reminding her that she had made a mistake. As far as the public knows (to this very day), the minister was very careless and created a situation very embarrassing to all who were present. This was something that could not be shared with anyone. Even though it was what we might call a road hazard in public travels, no one could sue another for damages. It was one of those burdens that must be borne as a result of one's agreeing to serve others in the company of community participants.

My First Memorial Service

Nothing has left an imprint on my memory equal to that of my first memorial service, one week before enrolling in college and immediately following my first Sunday of ministerial responsibilities. I had known some fearful times before. There had been a near-disaster at sea, some distance from the island of Saipan, during which the liberty ship Tazewell floated out of control for several hours. During an unrelenting storm, there was a near collision with another ship. There had been a tidal wave in the Pacific Ocean, causing much damage and creating danger all of the way from Hawaii to my seaside location in the Philippine Islands. The wind and waves nearly engulfed our shore camp area and seriously threatened our safety, almost forcing an evacuation. There had been constant excursions in which death was very likely. On one occasion, a typhoon moved into our location, and coconuts rained down like hail in a windstorm. It became my responsibility to dash through a storm-tossed coconut grove to release a man from protective custody.

Some of these events are stamped very vividly upon my memory, but nothing has ever caused me to feel as much uneasiness as did my first funeral service. I was not too disturbed by the idea of speaking before the public or the responsibility of delivering an appropriate eulogy for the occasion. However, I felt it would not be right for me to conduct the service because I was not yet an official minister in the church. I had no formal preparation for such a position. I questioned the judgment of the district superintendent, who had given me this assignment, and the soundness of my mentality for accepting it. It just seemed so improper.

I called on the bereaved family and made all of the necessary preparations for the service, which was scheduled for the next day. The night between was long and threatening. Finally, the day arrived. With my wife, I drove to the small but very attractive church in the Johnson Grove community, arriving a few minutes early. Many people were already waiting inside, but I could hardly persuade myself to enter and await the arrival of the funeral procession. I thought my own pastor, who had shown some strong interest in me up to this point, might also be present. If he comes, I'll promise him a thousand dollars to speak at this service and never again will I get caught in such a predicament. But he did not make an appearance, and I had to go in.

The pulpit loomed ominously before me—much as the electric chair must appear to one who is about to pay the supreme price for a crime committed against society. Even to this day, I have a mental image of that sanctuary as it appeared then. I heard car tires rolling on the fresh white gravel that was in front of the church and in the parking lot, and I knew the hour of destiny had arrived. Because of my distress, I was glad the wait was over. The front door opened, and the funeral director eased the carriage down onto the floor. Their feet shuffled as the attendants carefully moved into place. My near-hysterical mood vanished long enough for me to lead the congregation in a service of worship. Viewing the large number of people assembled—in and around the church-school rooms, the aisles, and everywhere else that a chair could be placed—I felt that all of the people of Crockett County had come to either pay their respects to the departed or witness the speaker vanish.

I was quite elated with the peace I experienced during the service. I was encouraged by the sincere and generous remarks extended to me after the service by many people who knew that this was my first such undertaking. The president of the local bank was present. A few weeks ago, he told me that he has remembered that service for all of these years. I casually reminded him that I have also. The service went well, but when leaving the church, I told Christine that she would have to drive; I was not able to do so.

Several years later, I returned for another funeral. I lived 20 miles away and was expected to go directly to the church. It was near the time the service was to begin. I felt sure the funeral procession had already left the funeral home in Alamo, some eight miles away. I discovered that my new suit had become divided at the rear, below the belt. Mr. Jack Tomlin, a member of this church, operated a general store that was nearby. He was helping a customer when I arrived. He was anxious to speak, shake hands, and go through the normal process of old friends meeting again after having been apart for several years, but I came quickly to the point. "Never mind the familiar friendly greetings, etc. Just give me a needle and thread and show me the way to the bathroom."

"Here is a needle and thread, but I don't have a bath-room here in the store," he answered. "Just get over there behind that high stack of merchandise and sew them up." I quickly returned the double-threaded needle to the clerk. "Did you get them fixed?" he asked.

"Yes, but I'm sure they must appear much as the story goes that tells about the monkey sewing up the elephant with the log cabin. It may not look so well, but it sure is stout."

As I relate these incidents, I recall many different individuals who helped me in many different situations. I find it to be nothing less than marvelous that when one is in desperate need, there are usually those around him who are more than willing to help turn disaster into harmony and defeat into victory. This is important for me to remember because the phone rang while I was writing these words. A very good friend of mine was just killed by a train, and I have been requested to return to the church in Halls and conduct the memorial service. Memory does not preserve all of my experiences, but hopefully the most important ones are remembered and recorded for future reference and daily encouragement.

A Stressful Benediction

One's ministry or helpfulness to others is seldom confined to the area of one's chosen profession. One should be alert to the needs of others as they arise in the normal course of daily activities. Dedicated citizens of a good society are often called upon to deploy helpfulness in the most unusual places and at the least expected times. This is very important because, unfortunately, there are individuals and groups who capitalize on the misfortunes of others.

In January 1971, I found myself playing the roles of policeman and minister at the funeral service of my brother-in-law, Keith Huston. Family members had been summoned to Bardville, Illinois, to be with relatives during this special time of loss and sorrow. I had agreed to conduct the memorial service the next day. I arrived there at noon on the day before the service, and we went directly to the funeral home.

The establishment was one of unique quality and attractiveness. Attendants in matching uniforms, wearing white dress gloves, served as doormen. The individual rooms were large and stately. I learned later from the proprietor, Wilber Foxgate, that he had come to this country at the close of World War II. He was a large man, very alert, and took great pride in the fact that he was 80 years of age and could still do his work in an expert fashion. His associates were also well trained and disciplined in the affairs of the business. The next day, Mr. Foxgate and I rode together to the cemetery. He said, "The Lord has surely been good to me since I came to America and established this business."

I wanted to say, "Yes, and I'm quite sure that the people of this city and geographical area have also been good to you."

The previous evening, as we met to discuss plans for the service, I began to question this man's honesty and integrity The family of the deceased had informed me there was a chapel in the cemetery, and that it could be used for delayed interment. After the benediction to the service, the carriage could be rolled down a ramp to a basement level compartment for storage. Later, when the weather was suitable, the casket could be carried to the grounds and buried. But my sister-in-law had secured a different arrangement with the funeral home.

The next day, the sun was shining, even though it had

snowed the night before. There were no windows in this
building. The carpet on the floor served to cushion the
walk and silence the acoustics of the entire building. The
chapel was located in the midst of several acres of groves
and cross-sectioned drives. It was just as isolated from the
public as it was attractive to those who happened to view
it.

Mr. Foxgate advised me that the funeral service would
be held at the funeral home chapel and the committal and
benediction would be said at the chapel in the cemetery.
"You will ride out there with me in my car, but you will return with the family as soon as the service is concluded."

I wondered about the arrangement. If I go out there in
his private car, why can't I return in like fashion? His vehicle certainly won't be crowded. But there was another
unusual angle to this situation. The deceased was being
buried in a very expensive solid-copper casket. This
caused me to be very sensitive to details and statements.

I suppose that if one has been a policeman, then he
will always have a certain degree of curiosity about unusual details. At least three times, I was informed of the
exact procedure to be used in going to and from the place
of burial. This man was rather crafty in conversation, but
by this time, I was completely certain that there was a
well-planned case of grave robbery in progress. I imagined
the words my kinsman would have said had he been able
to speak, "Don't let him do it. Stay with me! Don't turn
your back on me. It's up to you. We married sisters, boy,
you owe me something."

The funeral procession, which consisted entirely of
three business personnel, the family car, and the cars of
other close relatives, drove to the cemetery and stopped
within a few feet of the chapel door. The director advised

the widow that the family could return to the gravesite after one hour and view the arrangement of flowers. Another question came to my mind. If he is going to carry this casket directly from the chapel to the grounds, then why is he dismissing the hearse as soon as the funeral party enters the chapel? How will the last 500 yards be traveled?

While those present were taking their seats, I calculated that it would take the director about 30 minutes to return to the funeral home, which was downtown, pick up what he was going for—a wooden box, I suspected—and return to complete the arrangements before the family arrived at the grave. The chapel would have been a perfect place for the family to await completion of the interment, but that was not a part of the plan.

After the benediction was pronounced, the family left immediately. I whispered to my wife that I was going to stay. When she persisted to know why, I answered, "I'll tell you later." I stood near the end of the casket. When the others were gone, the chapel was very quiet. I didn't know what to expect. Up to this moment, everything had been accomplished with a great deal of perfection and accord. When I refused to leave the chapel, the owner of the business fell apart emotionally. He turned and strode out the entrance. His second-in-command followed quickly in his footsteps. That left only two of us in the chapel, including my late brother-in-law. I suddenly felt spooky and greatly outnumbered.

Only once before, that same day, had I ever felt as much out of place as I did then. When the prelude to the service began, I was obeying orders for me to remain at the rear of the chapel until I was told to go forward and begin the formal service. This same large, tall, and distin-

guished individual paused beside me. I looked up at him to
see what was happening. His stature made my 5-foot-11-
inch frame look like a nubbin left on a corn stalk after two
good ears had been pulled off. A little further into the prelude, a white satin glove, covering a hand as large as a
small ham of meat, grabbed me by the arm, and away we
went. How was I to know that he was going to escort me in
this fashion down the aisle to the podium? I had seen fathers escort daughters down the aisle in such a manner on
their wedding day, but a man escorting a man in this
fashion on the occasion of a funeral was something new
for me. I felt as though I were being arrested.

After waiting a short time, I took a quiet stroll back up
the aisle to see what the attendants were doing. Outside
the entrance, they had their heads together, with their
backs toward me. They did not know that I had left the
altar and was now hearing their conversation. I heard the
owner say, "He's not going to leave. What are we going to
do?"

His aid answered, "We had better send someone over
to the far side of the cemetery and see if we can get those
workmen to bring their truck over here and help us get to
the gravesite." Since there was no one to send other than
the minister or the 80-year-old owner of the business, he
went himself.

While hasty plans were being finalized, I said to these
two, "I'll be sitting here in your car until this job is completed." It was done in short order, but seeing a large
copper casket bumping up and down on a dirty, ragged
flatbed truck was in strange contrast to everything that
had transpired up to that point.

We had a very quiet ride back to the center of the city.
None of the beforehand bragging and mentioning of bless-

ings, which only came in America, were discussed on the return trip. I had the opinion that my position exceeded that of the funeral director at the time. The thought also came to me that I was probably the only $6,000 passenger in the history of the taxi business. I was addressed only once while we traveled. "Was the deceased related to you?"

My answer was short and to the point. "Yes, he was my brother-in-law."

It was clear from the very beginning that the copper casket was not doomed for burial that day, but when I heard it spelled out in simple English, I could hardly believe what I heard. I was the only observer who witnessed the event at the grave. I did all that I could have done. I conducted the service and then refused to leave until the final act was over. A good verse for describing those proceedings is "Let us be careful, lest our sins find us out" (Numbers 32:23).

Uncaptured By Adversity

Adversities should never stand in the way of new beginnings. Sympathizing with failure does little to encourage release from the enslavement of negative experiences and depreciating hopes for personal maturity. Once, Moses stood beside his people on the borders of a new land and admonished the children of Israel to remember all that they owed to God and to let their prevailing mood be one of thanksgiving. The Old Testament prophet was anxious to remove from his associates the disastrous attitude of pitying themselves.

On one occasion, one of my five brothers plainly conveyed to me this type of message. We were discussing a social situation, and I stated that needless aggravation was being directed to me personally by one who sought to annoy my peace of mind and hinder my efforts of service in the local church. I had made a statement concerning self-appointed disturbers of pastoral persuasions fostering their selfish egos. I was surprised by—but accepted in good faith—his reminder that some members of our family were prone to carry chips on their shoulders, including him. He further stated that this had not always been the case for me, but it appeared that some departure had been made from this type of practice. I extended a courteous reply of appreciation for his personal interest on my behalf, and little more was said concerning this issue. I was aware that my brother was telling me that I should be more grateful for the good things that had happened to me and that I should not attempt to major in minors.

I learned another important lesson, late one busy and hectic day, from my teenage daughter, whom I have always admired for many reasons especially for her outstanding ability to accept and see value in people of all ages and stations of living. I had reluctantly agreed to hold a funeral service for someone who was not associated with a church. After the conversation, I said, "That's the way with a good many folks. They don't have anything to do with the church until they die, and then they want someone to say nice things about them." Then came a true and penetrating reply from my own flesh-and-blood.

My daughter said, "If that had been one of your fine friends, you would not have said a word."

Often, the truth is not what we want to hear, but that does not remove the importance of hearing it. My reply was what any sensible person would have said. "You are exactly right. I'll hold the service." I have officiated at every service for which I have been requested, except two:

178

once when I was sick and in bed, and once when I was already scheduled to do one at the same hour.

These conversations are symbolic of many others that have been offered for my personal good over the years by family members and trusting friends. Others could be told, but these two are offered as a kindly tribute to my mother and father, five brothers, two sisters, and approximately 40 other relatives, but especially, to my wife, daughter, her husband, and their two-and-one-half-year-old son, Clay, who calls me Pop. He, no doubt, is the only person in the entire world who feels that Pop can do no wrong.

Until some adverse condition threatens to change our lifestyles, we may not appreciate our families as we should. We usually just take one another for granted, secure in the attitude that, should all else fail, we would still have the understanding, approval, and acceptance of the family unit. But no one is immune from various forms of tragedies.

While we were living in Covington, I returned home late one evening and found that our home had been damaged by a tornado. The roof of the house was extensively damaged, and a large tree in the yard had been uprooted and thrown across the garage. The car was inside. This was a fearful sight, but no one was hurt. It was an effective reminder that danger is not always so far away.

This skirmish with nature was a minor event compared to one that followed in the next week. My wife, daughter, and I were suddenly awakened in the late hours of the night by the destruction of the front door of our home. An intruder, who had already spent two terms in the state penitentiary for attacks on members of the opposite sex and who was eventually permanently confined as a habitual criminal, had invaded our home. For the following 45 minutes, human life truly hung in the balance. Later, many questions and facts were combined to formulate an answer to what motivated this tragic event.

At the time, I lived in the Tabernacle community near Covington, Tennessee. One of the three churches I was serving at the time was located across the street from our residence. A security light beside the church lit up my yard and front entrance to the house. The local general store was located just beyond the church—some 300 yards away. The attacker lived a few miles away and frequently passed by en route to Covington. On that Friday morning, all the men of Tabernacle, with the exception of one older man and me, had assembled at the store before leaving for a weekend fishing trip. The intruder happened to stop there while the arrangements were being made. He probably thought that I was going on the fishing trip. He believed that only my wife and daughter were at home that night.

Within a few seconds after the door was reduced to shambles, I came off the bed and grabbed an unloaded shotgun that had been placed in the corner of the room that very day. I could hear someone fast approaching my bedroom door, and my thoughts instantly reverted back to my military training—bayonet procedures, in particular. I assumed that only a person who was armed would break down a door, and I thought our only chance for survival was the element of surprise, which must be provided as I turned the corner leading to the living room. Suddenly, I was confronting an individual who appeared to have all of the necessary qualifications to compete on a professional basketball team. His strength and alertness complemented his physique. The opening where the front door had been was directly behind him. The light from outside allowed me to view this individual. His arms were extended and somewhat raised. It was evident to me that these protruding limbs, scrambling to make contact with his unexpected host, were the only weapons he commanded. Before physical contact was made, I pretended that the short-barreled bird gun was loaded and ordered the determined intruder to leave. He completely ignored this order. Even when I told him I would shoot him if he did not leave the house, he still paid no heed. I ended the struggle with a horizontal butt stroke to his rib cage. This lick brought about his running, staggering exodus through the shambles of what had once been a locked storm door.

But once he was outside the house, the trouble was not over. An hour passed before the sheriff arrived. In order to obtain more of an advantage over the intruder, I forced him to lie in a prone position. Even then, he made three desperate attempts to grab the gun from my hands. By this time, I happened to remember exactly where I had placed some extra ammunition for the weapon. I made a quick dash to retrieve this extra protection, and I was able to return before he could leave the yard. The clicking of the weapon as it was loaded brought the first renewed attack.

"You are going to kill me, so you might just as well do it," he remarked as he rushed very near to the end of the gun barrel.

"Please, don't make me do this. You are committing suicide," I replied. He quickly flopped to the ground. Three times this incident was repeated, and three times I was on the verge of shooting him. Fortunately, the sheriff finally arrived. But we had many sleepless nights afterwards.

Another tragedy happened 12 years later, in January 1977. This event was different in nature but very threatening to the security of my home and costly in many different ways. At the time, we resided in Halls, which is about midway between Dyersburg and Ripley, in Tennessee. There was sickness among my wife's family members in Memphis, some 60 miles south of our residence. Christine decided that she would attend church school that Sunday morning, then pick up our daughter, who lived in Ripley, and visit her ailing aunt.

The first part of the service had been completed. I had read a scripture lesson and raised my eyes to face the congregation and preach the sermon. A uniformed policeman approached the pulpit and motioned for me to join him. I wondered what I had done to merit this interruption of the worship service. He led me outside the church and informed me that there had been a wreck. He stopped speaking after making that comment. I suspected the worst.

"How bad?" I inquired.

"Real bad," he answered. "It was your wife."

"Is she living?"

"Yes, but they have carried her to the hospital."

"Which one?"

"To the hospital in Dyersburg."

I returned to the sanctuary and informed the congregation of what had happened and that I would have to leave. Some friends accompanied me to the hospital. At the moment we arrived, an ambulance turned into the emergency lane of the driveway. The driver confirmed that he had come from the wreck in which my wife was involved. When the door to the ambulance was opened, I was the first one to enter. There on a stretcher, lay a completely blanketed figure. I had seen too many such sights. I could reasonably draw only one conclusion—the worst had happened.

I moved to the other side of the stretcher and saw the face of a lady whom I did not know. "This is not my wife. Where did the other ambulance go?" I inquired, in a bit of haste and confusion.

"It went to Ripley," replied the attendant.

We quickly returned to the car, retraced the route back by the church, and then proceeded to the other hospital. During all of that time, I had no idea whether Christine was alive or dead. I went immediately to the emergency room. The door was open, and I could see that she was alive and being cared for by the hospital staff. It was not until several hours later that I knew the outcome for Mrs. Phillips Perkins. She, too, recovered—after many weeks of hospitalization.

We may not properly appreciate our family before some threatening situation arises. And, too, we may not fully experience the impact of joy until a danger has been eliminated. Adversities often create negative conditions, but hopefully, most can be used to produce positive results.

Ministerial Immorality

Ministerial immorality does not lend itself to pleasant discussion. Nevertheless, it is an issue of much concern to Christians. The ministerial image has suffered quite noticeably during the past several decades. The responsibility for this must be shared by all of society. Both clergy and nonclergy have contributed to the erosion of the moral stability and the public image of the ministerial profession.

The general public has a way of setting standards that are easily reached. We are prone to be more courteous than honest when considering the character of individuals with whom we wish to be compared. The Bible plainly teaches us that there was only one perfect person—Christ Jesus. We are also aware that His example demands unlimited obedience (if proper results are to be obtained). And, since we never give 100 percent of ourselves to anyone or anything, we are prone to seek other examples-people whose lives prove less challenging for us to emulate. Thus, a minister is often chosen as a pattern by which one lives his life. Such a practice results in disillusionment. The result has been that of constructing personal images and then disliking that which we have formulated. All of us have had the pleasure of knowing many ministers who have been very faithful to their moral and Christian trusts and who have shown no deceptive characteristics in any area of human association. This is as it should be, but something needs to be said about individuals who have been involved in behavior that hurt others and the Church.

What are some of these things, and how did they happen? Were all of these people "wolves in sheep's clothing"? Or did they lose their power to resist various forms of evil? There are some considerations (in no way meant to excuse immoral behavior) that may help to explain the disease of moral fatigue.

First of all, after all of the daily incidentals have been put to rest; after the public itch has been scratched in order to make everyone socially comfortable; after every effort has been made to oil the social machinery of hundreds of different personalities and temperaments, as well as treading softly upon opposing theological impressions; there is little time or energy left for the pastor of a church to devote to the chief purpose of his personal calling—that of preparing and preaching sermons that truly represent the Good News. A statement by Ralph W. Sockman in his book, *Paradoxes of Jesus*, is very descriptive of those who have sought not to compromise their noble principles. "It is the characteristic of good men that the better they are, the more conscious they are of their shortcomings."[20]

A second form of ministerial oppression occurs when a sensitive pastor is bothered by hypocritical piety to the extent that he actually desires a flirtation with evil as a diversionary tonic to soothe a thirsting soul. Society helps to make a public servant, but it may also help to break those whom it has composed. The institutional church is not completely innocent of this evil.

A decent person wants to be decent because he wants to be that way, not because someone demands that he be that type of individual. No one enjoys forced righteousness. Nowhere is this more evident than in the minds and hearts of children born and reared in the homes of short-sighted members of the Christian ministry who are blind to the individual needs and welfare of their own children. Many parsonage children grow into adulthood secretly resenting their fathers for baby-sitting their congregation's children while leaving their own to forage for themselves. These children feel that they have become pawns or public items to be used to bolster the congregation's image of their pastor. Instead of children being loved and appreciated within a family unit, they become tools to be used for community expediency. This is one of the reasons that many children who are reared in pastoral homes grow up resenting the church and much of what it teaches.

Christian hypocrisy can be very damaging to the sensitive faiths of Christians who are young in the faith. It also places a heavy burden upon mature Christians. When the heart is absent from one's ministerial activities, the will becomes a tardy servant. Christian response that is born out of public compulsion leaves one spiritually empty and void of moral sentiment.

Many church members are aware that congregations place a great deal of pressure on their ministers. Many times, a member has said to me, "Well, preacher, you can't please them all. Just do the best you can and leave it at that." Unfortunately, too many of those times, demanding members who often sought special recognition and liberties were the ones to say it. There is no legitimate reason for a church member to expect favoritism from his pastor. I do not feel the least irreverent when I say, "Lord, have mercy upon the pastor who happens to have as his ultimate goal the pleasing of every Tom, Dick, and Harry in the local church."

I have yet to become acquainted with a congregation where every member is 100 percent Christ-like in thought and example. Hypocrisy is a very dangerous matter for Christians and churches.

A third factor, which fosters ministerial weakness, involves maladjustments on the part of a minister. Spiritual fatigue is debilitating. It is a common result of prolonged pressures and will result in internal moral combustion unless healthy release is obtained. The illness is often overlooked until the symptoms become apparent to others.

Attention is called to the often-repeated statements: I'm shocked at his conduct; I would never have thought that of him; he seemed to be a person of unquestionable integrity; I have come to realize that they are all alike; they just play the righteous game and all the while are companions of evil. Individuals of a chosen profession are not all alike, and all persons serving the church are not alike. All receive the same invitations to do wrong, but not all transgress the bonds of common good and community trust.

Those who serve the church as laymen are not always as virtuous as they may appear to be. On one occasion, a member of my pastoral committee, Joseph Pickens, refused to report a voted increase in pastoral salary but at the same time offered a few cents discount on items I purchased in his store. I believe he did so to demonstrate that I was subject to the authority of the members.

There are individuals (often, obscured from the church at large) who use some rather refined trickery in attempts to get a pastor to view himself as less than he actually is. Yet, whatever the reasons may be, sin is the result and reward. The same sins manifested through different individuals still have the same negative degrading results.

A double standard is worse than no standard at all. Such a system seeks to excuse one and condemn another. The regulating norms for the minister must also bear upon the conduct of each member of the church. The sins of any member hurt the church as a body. No matter who the guilty party is, the results have a negative impact upon all concerned.

I feel that one should never be too anxious to criticize his minister. There is no such thing as a separate ministerial immorality; sin is sin—whether it involves private or public conduct of a sinful nature.

Social Tragedies

Early in my ministry, I discovered that many religious attitudes are not the result of strong theological discipline. The more I become associated with people in work and worship, the more evident it becomes to me that church attendance does not guarantee Christian conduct.

Henry Hudson was not a church member. At the time I
met him, he was not attending church anywhere but later
showed some interest in this matter. This change in attitude came after Henry and I had begun to enjoy occa-
sional fishing trips together. On various occasions, while
waiting for the fish to bite, he would question me concerning issues of the Christian faith and the church in
particular. He attended a few worship services and indicated that he enjoyed them.

This was not an easy change for Henry. He had been
reared in what he called "a rough and rugged environment." The rural farming area where he lived as a youth
had social customs that were quite different from those of
our community. I believed that my friend had an inferi-
ority complex because of the poor standard of living he experienced during those challenging years.

An interesting episode of his earlier life was related to
me—a conversation he overheard between two of his associates. The employee was new, not to the industry of agriculture and plowing with mule teams, but to this farm and
his current employer. The landlord, speaking to the
tenant, said, "I am an unusual person. I have my own way
of doing things. I curse a lot and call my employees all
sorts of names. Someday, I may come out here and curse
you out for no apparent reason. When I do, I don't want
you to think a thing about it. This is just my way."

The employee waited until he had finished his speech
and then replied, "Yes, and when I take the singletree off
that plow and knock your brains out with it, I don't want
you to think a thing about it. That will just be my way of
doing things." That was Henry's way of describing something of the nature of his earlier employment.

The nature of some of the subjects we discussed as we

waited for the fish to strike was consistent with what was
once conveyed to me by his wife, who was very active in
the local church and the community in general. "Henry
asked me the other day where God came from. When I
was slow to answer, he said, 'That's all right. I'll ask the
preacher. He'll know.'"

We suddenly became estranged. Henry confided in me
that someone in the church had publicly complained
about his minister associating with that Henry Hudson.
"Did you know that they are actually fishing together?"
When Henry was honestly and clearly reminded that this
type of crude gossip should have no effect on our friendship and recreational activities, he seemed somewhat re-
lieved. But, never again did he attend a service of worship.
I consider this to have been the cruelest act I am aware of
that affected the awakening faith of someone who had
given evidence that he was about ready to know and practice a different way of life.

In religion, as well as in casual conversation, there is a
"time to speak and a time to remain silent; there is a time
to laugh and a time to cry" (Ecclesiastes 3:7). Everything
that is said and done in the name of religion is not Christ-
like in nature. This lasting memory involving my friendship with Henry causes me a great deal of sadness. I feel it
would be very good if all could remember and apply the
words of Jesus, "He that is without sin among you, let him
first cast a stone at her" (John 8:7).

Dynamics of Growth

The mental, moral, physical, and spiritual growth of a
person does not happen without effort, nourishment, and
cultivation of personal virtues and endowments. One is
born with a basic potential for maturity, but maturation

depends upon the development of all of his available faculties. The life and worth of any person cannot be properly
judged from the standpoint of his origin, but rather, his
destination. Abraham Lincoln once said, "I don't even
know who my grandfather was, but I am much more concerned about who his grandson becomes."

Individual growth is affected by many factors, including memory, friendship, embarrassment, and even
tragedy—influences in every life. Thus, every person is a
product of successes and failures, joys and sorrows.
"There is a little good in the worst of us, and a little bad in
the best of us."

Many different items of personal interest have been
noted in these pages. In each case, I have sought to create
a bit of "sunshine," even for those times of gloom. Memory
is the by-product of experience, and when I consider the
events I have experienced, I am reminded that life is no
joke, and I do not wish to leave the impression that we
can laugh our troubles away. However, I am saying we
should not make situations worse than they actually are. I
am very much aware that our chores and daily routines
can set our lives adrift upon the sea of dull experience. So
difficulties—especially for Christians—can challenge us
and contribute to our growth. Even our best friendships
are often tested. When friendships are strained by circumstance, new channels of communication and expression
must come forth; otherwise, we become wards of our own
solitude. For this very reason, many anxious people are
repeating in their thoughts the words of an old folk song:
"Where Is That Place Called Lonely Street?" It is so often
located in the heart and mind of the inquirer.

Friendship is a dividend of mutual participation. It is a
reward for unselfish sharing of common virtues, but when

channels of communication become closed, negative results are evident. The faithful wife, mother, and friend who moves out of the home to mingle in a more diverse mode of social activity often creates a sense of estrangement, deceit, and discord in the mind of a compassionate husband and devoted father. And a feeling of being deserted prevails in the minds and moods of maturing children, brought on by tensions for which they are not responsible. Many marriages have been destroyed because one partner became lonely and bored.

Embarrassment is characterized by a sense of failure. Its symptoms are almost always related to a fear of rejection. While in the Philippine Islands, Sergeant Edward Buehler and I were assigned the task of delivering two long-term prisoners to an institution that was 200 miles from our base at San Fernando. We arrived late in the evening and had our evening meal with the personnel of the prison—the likes of which I had never seen before and hope to never see again. Three thousand inmates (the results of the rigors of war) were confined in one small area of human existence. My friend and I thought it would be enjoyable to attend one of their sports events. It was already in progress by the time we had finished our meal. We had begun to walk the short distance to the bleachers before we realized that we were considered unwelcome by this vast wall of humanity dressed in prison attire.

We later concluded that our uniforms, which represented our freedom, caused embarrassment for those who were confined. A chant of nonacceptance began with a few voices calling out and suddenly became a boisterous roar. As we drew near, the crowd became almost hysterical. One of us said to the other—I don't know which one of us spoke—"If we want to live, we had better quickly retrace our steps and get out of this compound." If one has never heard such personal threats coming from so many people, he can't properly appreciate our sense of utter smallness and fear. This was an extreme case of resentment and embarrassment, created by the each man's failure to abide by the laws protecting the rights of all concerned.

We should always remember tragedies, even though tragedy interrupts individual happiness. When tragedy occurs during the pursuit of a goal, it mars our sense of attainment. It tries our faith and sense of fairness because it is often the result of an unjustified encroachment by someone upon the rights and welfare of others. While en route to the prison, Sergeant Buehler and I had a silent ride along the infamous Bataan Death March route. This was a never-to-be-forgotten experience for me. Just to travel this lonely road, where a few months before so many gave their last ounce of energy and lifeblood to satisfy the brute passions of their victors, reminded me that this should never be forgotten by a civilized society. Memory serves to bless us, but the failure to remember so often aids our condemnation.

Much human tragedy is self-imposed. In order to help dispel periods of gloom, frustration, and weariness, some friends and I, who were stationed on Base M, near the seacoast at San Fernando, obtained a small boat for close-in rides upon the water. The motor was old and not as dependable as it should have been for such a dangerous place of recreation. It was hard to start, but if one persisted, it would usually run.

Late one evening, I decided to spend a few minutes taking a short ride alone. No one knew of my intention; I was strictly on my own. The waves were reasonably calm, but, unknown to me, the tide was going out. During my few minutes of cranking and rocking back and forth, I never once noticed I was drifting from shore. When I finally gave up my efforts to start the motor, I looked up to step out on the shore and was startled. The tide had moved me outward a long distance on the South China Sea. My first concern was to find a paddle. I discovered part of a board, about two feet in length. I am completely convinced that I owe my life to that small piece of timber. The boat was heavy and difficult to paddle, but I got on my knees and began to work for dear life—and that's just what my efforts amounted to. At first, there was no movement, but eventually the boat slowly moved toward shore. After reaching a place where I thought wading would be possible, I dropped over the side and out of sight into the rolling sea. I swam to the surface, grabbed my wobbling seagoing vessel and began my laboring once again. I debarked upon the sandy soils of Northern Luzon. The title of an old song I had often heard sung in my home church came to mind: "You Are Drifting Too Far From the Shore."

My compensation for a near-tragic decision was my trip aboard the army transport the William M. Weigel as it crossed San Fernando harbor on the way home to America. One of my thoughts as our ship departed that island was that life is precious but we often threaten our well-being with those things that seem so unimportant at the time.

There are many events in life; some make us happy, and some cause us sadness. I sincerely believe that the joys available to us all should help to dispel the lonely and trying occasions that come to all of us. No, life is not one large joke. It is a very serious matter, and it calls for the very best in everyone to help make it better for all concerned. If my humble ministry in the church can aid this noble cause, then all of my efforts and the efforts of the many people who have helped me so much will not have been in vain.

Chapter Fourteen

A Stereotyped Society

Many members of society have become champions in the stereotyping of an individual based upon professional identity. This is a tragedy. Such dogmatic opinions and creeds leave little room for renewed thought, personal social development, and the acceptance of other people possessing opposing values. This poses an unnecessary and immoral burden upon society by creating various tensions. I believe that many people are unaware of the dangers and oppressions placed upon the general public as a result of unyielding impressions and intentions that are derived from self-centeredness.

Sensitive persons often give serious thought to conditions that depreciate the common good. Some time ago, an area newspaper carried a public real estate advertisement that created enough interest for my wife and me to make an appointment to view the property that was being offered for sale. We were riding with a company representative to see the property, but the trip ended abruptly after he asked some questions. "I have been in this business a long time. Will you give me an answer today concerning your interest to buy? What business are you in anyway?" When I told him I was a minister, the trip was suddenly terminated.

While we were returning to company headquarters, our host made another unprofessional statement: "There are four professions that I find hard to deal with, and the ministry is one of them. The others are engineers, accountants, and lawyers." I had the uneasy feeling that I did not fit the profile that qualified me for successful financial endeavors. This clinging to preconceived opinions may well have cost that individual a sale.

Some two years ago, I was summoned for prospective jury duty in the circuit court of the county in which I resided. An assortment of public and private offenses had been affirmed by the local grand jury, including one defined by civil statute as a capital offense. It was the only case in which the state was seeking the death penalty—contingent upon the jury's verdict of guilty. For nearly a week, my name was called. Then questions followed about my preconceived opinions concerning guilt, fairness based solely on evidence presented, and other issues of civil concern. The interview for each juror concluded with a dismissal by the defense.

This went on each day of court until the final case came to trial. This happened to be the one pertaining to the capital offense charge, and it was evident that the court had very nearly exhausted its roll of perspective jurors. I happened to notice that one name was added to the list and later discovered it was mine. I was called once again to the stand, and the same basic questions were repeated. I was the last person to be selected for the jury that would hear that case. Prior to this, I asked the judge to release me from the daily calling of the roll because it appeared to me that a minister was considered inappropriate for this type of civic duty. The judge replied, "Russell, just come on back. We enjoy having you around."

The case was tried, and conviction was obtained. The court was adjourned. It was then that the defense attorney sought a private conversation with me. "You have been the subject of much behind-the-scene debate here this week. We couldn't decide whether or not a minister would be able to sit in judgment upon this type of case and not be persuaded by his private opinions of right and wrong and fail to render a verdict based solely upon evidence presented in court."

I rendered my response with a degree of internal embarrassment and outward defense of my chosen profession. "I would desire that members of the ministry be viewed as persons with enough maturity, common sense, and respect for the civil law to function as responsible members of society. I did not enjoy the mammoth responsibility placed upon me in this case. Yet, I was aware that a decision had to be made. I realized I was no better for this role than anyone else."

I had the impression that I had been placed in one small area of human concern, and that I was not supposed to depart from it. I believe that if all individuals were to have concern and respect for professions other than their own, then it would be a great step forward in the creation of harmonious living for all concerned.

While attending seminary, I was asked to officiate at the funeral service of a member of a former church. There had been no previous warning of illness. The death was a shock to the entire family. I skipped an afternoon class and stopped off for the service en route home. This was on Monday. The following Thursday, the same request was made for the wife. She, too, passed away unexpectedly. At the funeral home, on the night before the second funeral, one of the family members caused me a great deal of anxiety and then a bit of elation.

"Do you know what you did when you were here four days ago for the service of my father-in-law?"

I began a quick review of what had happened and what had been said during the service. I could not recall anything that might have offended anyone.

The spokesman went on to say, "My brother-in-law, who lives in a distant city, happens to be a high official in a major automobile manufacturing company. He is a good man, but business is his life. He has no time for the church. He feels that it is very unimportant. His negative attitude in this matter has caused his mother a great deal of sorrow and fear for her son's spiritual welfare. However, he said after the first service that he found more meaning in those few common words spoken at the service than he had ever heard before. It had such an impact on him that he called his mother and related his new-found joy to her. He also reminded his daughter that they were going to church the following Sunday morning."

I feel that no excellence was demonstrated on my part. I have a personal desire to be very honest, responsible, and helpful to people on such stressful occasions. He developed a personal appreciation for the sincere efforts of one who had sought to help others in an acute time of need. My profession and his no longer seemed to be so far apart. Surely, both the building of automobiles and the reading of the Bible have a place of usefulness in every civilized society.

Fraternal Tensions

The student who never graduates and the destination that is never reached are symbolic of the minister's role in the traditional church. He begins the affairs of each new week without having completed the responsibilities and expectations of the one before it. Somehow, he must learn to endure this type of professional ambiguity. Perhaps, compliments for efforts extended are the most encouraging sustenance he can receive. But, according to some advice given by an experienced public servant to one who was just beginning his formal preparation for the Christian ministry, even praise or flattery must be accepted with caution. "Compliments are life's perfume; they are to be received but never swallowed."

Every pastor pauses and looks back at past experiences and looks forward to that which will probably become a reality. He asks questions like these: Can I ever justify the expense of releasing my mental privacy? Is it worth it? Can I afford to trample on the attitudes and emotions of others?

Personal ideas, opinions, and convictions project themselves into one's mission and message, and without these, the very best communication loses much of its interest. Yet, I find it rather hard to relate personal experiences that tend to be self-complimentary. I also dislike the type of sermonic rendition that portrays the speaker as an envied hero. Whether it is of a personal nature or an impersonal one, subject matter should be chosen with caution. Wise, indeed, is the spokesman who remembers that tensions are very easily created and alienation is often unnecessary. Emotional stability is worthy of careful consideration on the part of all concerned.

The structures of many denominations lend themselves to the formation of internal power struggles with far-reaching consequences. The delegation of authority sets the stage for the courting of delegates. During a recent conference, one lay-delegate, Joseph Pickens, who sought to be reelected as a delegate to a general conference, refrained from speaking on a tension-filled issue until his position in the matter had been secured. Relationships within the institutional church are often forged and cultivated based upon professional status. Many servants of the church may sum up their careers as "a ministry of moving." The individual who has as his most cherished ambition the holding of the highest paying parishes must always be ready to assume a new appointment with little consideration for anyone or anything. If he is willing to play the game of church politics, he is usually rewarded by monetary and prestigious favor. However, a sense of internal satisfaction seems forever to evade his fondest dreams, leaving the career-minded minister to flounder in a state of mental and spiritual frustration.

The appointment of one minister to the position of district superintendent resulted in personal strife for me. I believe he posed as an over-eager and commanding administrator because he was aware that many ministers in the conference had rejected his promotion. He contributed many positive things to the church as a whole but gave evidence of being unduly threatened by pastors whose ministry at local churches allowed them to remain in those appointments over extended periods of time.

My personal status as a minister and my future appointments were threatened by, and underwent a degree of damage from, the tension that existed between this official and the Pastor-Parish Relation Committee of my charge. At the beginning of the next conference year, I was given a choice about moving. When I made the decision to accept the recommendation of the pastoral committee and stay, my superintendent informed me that I might just stand on my own when appointments were made the following year. He also proceeded to notify other district superintendents that I would no longer receive his personal blessing. "As far as I am concerned, he has been offered a good appointment, but wouldn't accept it. For this reason, he has had it." Had it not been for others in administrative positions, his prediction might have been accurate.

His attitude toward me caused me to question my having spent seven and one-half years in the classroom, my first charge of three churches paying a combined salary of $1,700, the 350,000 miles I had traveled, and the three cars I had worn out during that time. But, some two years later, he offered an apology, and I accepted it. However, the truth still remains—that was one of the two most humiliating experiences of my life. It was truly not a time to laugh but more of a time to cry.

It is not just ordained clergymen who create strife in regard to ministerial appointments. Lay participation has quite frequently made negative contributions as well. On one such occasion, the nominating committee of my church held its regular meeting to nominate the church officials for the ensuing year, subject to the action of the Charge Conference. During the course of events, changes were made in the personnel. This prospect had not been mentioned to me. The decision was probably prompted by the opinions of three individuals, who, with my assistance, had prepared for our annual oyster dinner at the church one cold, January day.

We were sitting around a table talking before we began cooking. Some discussion followed pertaining to financial adversities. Without seeking or expecting any great deal of sympathy, I simply made the statement that the past week had not been a good one for me financially. They all wanted an explanation. I told these three church members that I had received word from the farm that 10 head of cattle had died from food poisoning and that the number was expected to increase. Not one additional word was said concerning this matter, nor was any sign of sorrow visible in the expressions of these three people, who were recognized by many as considerate and dependable members of their church. That night, I did not enjoy the oysters as much as I usually did.

The members of the church, with very few exceptions, were very gracious to my family and me. But I was saddened to learn that individuals could be as cold and unsympathetic regarding the welfare of others as these three had been toward me. Evidently, when the money was used to pay for my daughter's college expenses and my seminary expenses—incurred at the same time—it was acceptable to them for me to earn money from the sale of cattle. But, since we had both finished school, it was sinful for me to continue to earn any extra compensation. Also, I had reason to believe that other individuals resented my wife's working in a neighboring city. I wondered who had invented the idea that poor preachers make the best preachers.

I believe that every thoughtful person should be concerned not only about his own welfare but also about the livelihood of others. I do not believe it is God's intent for ministers to dispense kindness and not receive it. I think his plan was for kindness to be given and received by all.

Attempting to be involved only in those situations that are personally pleasing is a trait familiar to most people. One weekday afternoon, the United Methodist Women of our local church were meeting in the lovely home of one of the members. I had been invited to attend this session for the purpose of installing the newly elected officers. When I arrived, I entered the crowded living room through a side door and spoke at once, with a bow, to all present. There was much unofficial discussion going on at the time, and all present had not noticed my recent arrival. One lady turned and exclaimed, "Oh, we have a man present," which was pleasing to me. But, this pleasant greeting was doomed to short duration. Another lady took the initiative to set the record straight: "This is no man. He is a preacher."

Compelled to give a more appropriate identity for myself, I advised everyone that before one could be anything else, he had to first be a person and that it was my personal opinion that my ideas, likes and dislikes, and compulsions were those of a man. That clarification of my individuality brought laughter from some, but from others, it brought frozen expressions of non-appreciation and resentment.

Incidents such as this one led me to believe that institutional religion has closed in too closely on wholesome humor and called it evil. I am convinced there is a yet-to-be discovered area of human values that is well overdue for recognition—an area of thought that is, of itself, neither religious nor immoral. Pietistic views of morality that are expressed in straitjacketed molds of sermonizing, that dictate a somber expression of Christian values, and that consider most forms of entertainment to be morally wrong are rather appalling to many modern minds. This is why many young people refuse to be absorbed into the institutional church. "Just because we have always done it this way doesn't make a thing right or wrong."

Shortly after I was appointed to the church at Spencer, a fellowship dinner was in progress in the church dining room. The new pastor politely failed to respond to the urging of some to be served first. When I suggested that

the children be served first, Mrs. Ada Ikes became somewhat upset and resentful. This occasion was not soon forgotten. My sermons became unacceptable to her; to
entertain herself during the worship service, she began to
bring a book and to read it during the hour of worship.

Many people give strong evidence of having no intention of doing or experiencing anything apart from what
aids their desire to worship God. However, others often
give evidence that the same type of preparation for worship is a burden to them. I have little wonder why there is
an abundance of both joy and sorrow in church. If there
were to be more practicing of the biblical statement "Do
unto others as you would have them do unto you," then
many of the tragedies of working and worshipping with
others would be eliminated.

PART FOUR
REFLECTIONS

Chapter Fifteen

From My Point of View

Perhaps every story needs a change of venue. It is a long road that never turns. I wish to make a short detour at this point in my observations.

The story has been told about a large segment of church-related people who had gathered in one of our East Coast cities. People had come from many countries throughout the world. Various renowned individuals attended the convention. Most had served the Christian cause for many years.

At the beginning of the proceedings, a young man led the congregation in a worshipful devotion. (I wish to make it clear that I am not one to make light of anyone's religion or the manner in which he prays. I like to laugh *with* people, but not *at* them. I am simply repeating what I once read—with emphasis on one man's response.) The speaker began his prayer by asking God to be present with those who were assembled. His remarks sought to embrace people who had gathered from many parts of the world. As he prayed, his focus moved to the West Coast of the United States, crossed over the Asian countries, and continued with his mentioning of the people of South America and Africa. Then, he crossed over into Europe and began to set a course for New York City. At that point, someone on the dais leaned over close to the person seated beside him and whispered, "Thank the Lord. He is finally coming home."

Well, in this writing, I too am finally coming home, but I am not quite there yet. En route, I want to do some reflecting on some scenes already viewed on this long historical journey.

Fifteen years ago I retired from the ministry. A friend of mine became ill one Sunday and asked me to fill in for him. He recovered from his illness, but he never returned to his church position as a minister. It took me five years to leave that appointment. It was somewhat like a post-interlude to an earlier rendition. It was a good experience for me. There must have been a reason for that additional period of service. Maybe I was not as much of a finished product as some might have thought.

For the past 10 years, I have been retired from the ministry, but not from living. Shortly after retiring, I was seated in a doctor's waiting room for some sort of medical service, but I was not sick. I must have been waiting to get a flu shot. All I wanted was to get through and be on my way home.

The doctor's waiting room was small, and there were several other people waiting to see the doctor. Directly across from me sat a young mother with her youthful son. For some time, the boy, who was about four years of age, kept his eyes firmly fixed on me. He did not say a word to anyone. He just continued to stare at me, so I finally decided to speak to him. I had talked to many children in the churches I had pastored. I knew what the boy wanted.

He just wished I would say something to him. I knew I could handle the situation. I said, "Hi, Son. How are you this morning?" He did not tell me how he was, but he did express his feelings to his mother.

The child placed his mouth near his mother's ear. All the while, he kept his eyes very carefully fixed on me, and said, in a low but very audible voice, "Mother, there sits a very mean man over there." All who were present let out a comfortable laugh, including me. But, it did cause me to reflect. If I appeared to be stodgy, then I needed to loosen up and live.

Retirement has allowed me the time to do some serious thinking about the past as well as my plans for the future.

At this point in my life, I am led to consider the contributions that John the Baptist made in a formative period of his life. He was not a young man, but he held the opinion that he had a needful place in the affairs of humanity.

John resided in the desert of Judea. His food consisted of locust and wild honey, and he made his clothing from the coarse hair of wild animals. He was a rugged individual living in a primitive environment.

John constantly brooded over Scriptures, especially those involving Elijah's career. This primitive but profound religious scholar of the New Testament began his public ministry in the wilderness area of the country (Mark 1:4). The Jordan River was the main scene of his activity. He was devoted to admonishing people to reform their ways of living. He wanted people to recognize the responsibilities they had as a part of humanity.

John was the originator of the practice of baptism being performed as a symbol of Christian conversion. His theory was so profound that Jesus later affirmed it and began to advocate baptism as a sacrament of the Christian Faith. That pre-announcer of the coming of Christ was not received well by the elite, but the "common people heard him gladly" (Luke 7:29).

This is just one more reminder that servants come in many forms. As Dr. Gene Davenport once wrote, "The gospel itself concerns the call and use of ordinary people for extraordinary purposes of God" (Reid, 1983). John the Baptist fulfilled that role quite well. He gave his all, including his life, in order to convey his message of hope and salvation.

Since my retirement began, most of my reflections have originated while sitting in a church pew on Sunday during a worship service and while at the fish lake and on my tractor here on the farm, near Jackson, Tennessee. Sitting on a tractor seat, baling hay for my cattle's winter feed, and sowing wheat for cows and deer to graze provide me with special times of mental exercise.

Some people think I am too old for that kind of activity, but I'm prone to heed the remark of one good friend who said, "I had rather see you go while you are doing what you want to than to see you fall off the porch and kill yourself." That same person has given me much good advice over the years.

It was here on the farm that I decided to finish this book, which I began some 20 years ago. Until retirement, my time, efforts, and energy were spent in a structured life. I had little time to consider anything other than the immediate.

If some of these pages should yield a faint aroma of diesel fuel, it is because portions of this work originated while I was doing tractor work in the field. Yesterday, I was clipping some pastureland and trying to give some order to what I had already written when a change in subject matter became the order of the day. A swarm of yellow jackets greeted me in an unfriendly fashion. Three of them got past my defense and took their hostility out on me. My thoughts at the time were not very conducive to good manuscript composition. I was tempted to write a few lines about the subject "Devils in Disguise." Again, I had to put my mental efforts on hold.

I often spend time reflecting on past events of my church experience. This particular one stands alone at this time. Mrs. Anne Belle Carothers was church secretary, and had been for many years, at the Bethany Parkway Church in Memphis, Tennessee. She had witnessed the coming and going of many ministers and other people of her church.

Mrs. Anne Belle was in her 80s at the time of our service together. She was strictly a professional in matters of church administration. On one occasion, she informed me, "I will write your pastor's report if you want me to."

I replied, "No, thank you. I have to do something around here to earn my keep."

Mrs. Carothers lived alone. I believe her nearest relative was her daughter, and she lived in Texas. She drove her own car to work and anywhere else she wanted to go. During a time of ice and snow, she fell and broke her hip. She had to have surgery and was away from work for about three weeks. During that time of recuperation, I visited her and could tell she was very anxious to get back to work. The afternoon before she returned, I spoke to her on the telephone. She informed me she would be back at work the next morning. I replied, "I will come by and pick you up." My offer was declined.

She said, "Thank you, but I'll drive my car to the church." The next morning when I arrived, she was already there with her usual smile and "ready-to-do business" attitude.

Our offices were a good distance apart. There was a covered walkway from one part of the building to the other. I would usually go and greet her each morning and then return to my study.

During the first weeks of my tenure at that church, I continued to walk to her office each day to spend a few minutes with her in conversation. One day, she confronted me with these words: "I hope you do not come in here some morning and begin to chew me out for some reason or another!"

My response was, "If you are waiting for me to come over here and make an idiot of myself, you will be waiting a long time. I don't do business in that fashion. If I have some reason to discuss an issue with you, and if you have something you want to discuss with me, we will sit down and address the matter." From then on, we enjoyed a happy and effective relationship together.

Even when things were going well at a church, there were members who sought to throw a monkey wrench into the machinery of people business. At Bethany Parkway, one man requested not only that Mrs. Carothers be removed but also that she be replaced by a woman who had no experience in church administration. (I think she had experience, all right, but not in the area of church-related activities.) This individual approached me two or three times (seeking my efforts to make a change). That would have split the peace of that church from the ceiling to the floor. I clearly informed the individual that as long as I was the minister at that church, such would not be the case. I told the individual that Mrs. Carothers was very efficient in her work and of great help to me. To fire her would break her heart. The question of replacing Mrs. Carothers was resolved, and the answer was "no." Another church member informed me that the man wanting the change was not accustomed to having his request denied. I said, "The issue has been settled."

My co-worker was normally in a happy state of mind, and I could usually determine when a personal problem was bothering her. On such occasions, I would engage her in some semihumorous discussion. Almost without exception, I would leave her with a smile on her face and a twinkle in her eye.

One morning, I could tell she was disturbed, and I began my spiel. She soon lightened up and looked at me with her head slightly lowered, eyes protruding in my direction, and said with emphasis, "You are a rascal!"

Maybe, I am; maybe, I'm not. I suppose the truth lies in the eye of the beholder. I was most pleased with her humorous comment.

The only time Mrs. Anne Belle ever did something that aggravated me involved her response to a friend of mine from my former church. I was not in my office, and she attempted to discourage my good friend from calling back. She said, "The preacher is rather busy." I have never been too busy to take a call from a friend. I suppose everyone has an off day, now and then.

As I said earlier, one does not travel far on the road of life before he encounters both pros and cons in his affairs with other people. My current reflections are a combination of both. I often think about my first military police assignment, under a veteran policeman, Sgt. Bill Sitton. The results of that event have been very hard to ignore. Bill had been with the company since the army advanced up the Islands from New Guinea. He was strictly a combat veteran. This soldier was very careful when considering my safety as a rookie policeman.

There had been a shooting in a backward area outside the city of San Fernando. Two soldiers were visiting a house of ill repute when trouble developed. The brother of a social member of the institution shot one of the military visitors—killing him. He also sought to kill the other one but shot him through the tail of his shirt as he fled the scene. I imagine the soldier had a different outlook on life from that point on.

An emergency call came into the police station while my superior and I were on duty. Sgt. Sitton and I rushed to the scene of the crime. The last part of the trip could not be traveled by jeep, so we got out and wound our way on foot over a narrow wilderness trail. I can still hear the veteran soldier saying, "Reid, put a round in the chamber."

As it turned out, the ambulance attendants had already picked up the casualty and were gone when we arrived. The only person still in the area was the fellow with the torn shirt. By the time other emergency personnel arrived, including a commissioned officer, our only option was to hide in the nearby mosquito-infested swamp to catch the murderer if he returned.

My sergeant left with the others, but another soldier, whom I did not know, and I waited for some time, while the insects swarmed all over us. It was a miserable ordeal, but the worst was yet to come.

About 10 days later, I became critically ill. I spent a month in the hospital. The first two nights and days, I fluctuated in and out of consciousness. I had contracted dengue fever, which is an acute form of malaria. The only treatment known to the medical professionals was to administer Atabrine tablets on a daily basis for as long as I was in the tropical area of the world. It was affirmed that there was no cure available at that time.

About 20 people in my ward had the illness. A doctor came around once a day, and a nurse who carried a handful of pills followed him. The rest of the time, we were on our own—with one exception. One of the patients, a tall, handsome black soldier, really became our source of sustenance. I never knew what his medical problem was, for he did not appear ill.

This man waited on us hand and foot. It was most assuring to wake up in the middle of the night and see him looking down on me, checking on my well-being. That was a period when the military forces were not integrated. Later, I wondered how this man could have been so kind. There are a lot of good people in this world, and he is one of them. I hope that man has had a good and happy life.

Yes, some stories never seem to end. After my military discharge, I continued to suffer reoccurrence of the illness on an annual basis. For 25 years, the month of May was a disaster for me. My fever would nearly get out of control, I was nauseated, and my entire body was in pain. It appeared to get worse each year. Just for the record, the killer who caused my dengue fever was apprehended the day before I left the Philippine Islands, headed for home and my military discharge.

I became very fearful that my illness would shorten my life. I was most concerned that I might not survive to provide for my family. That condition really took a toll on my life for many years. It was no fun to wrap up in a large beach towel, treated with ice water, and sleep on the floor.

I'd get up in the morning and go to work. I would have to have been out of my mind to consider furthering my education at that point.

The bottom line of the story is that the immorality of two other people had a lasting negative effect on my family and me. I could be very bitter because of that imposition, but I'm just thankful to be alive. I often wonder how my swamp-partner came out of his ordeal.

I hasten to report the good news about that adversity. Some 30 years later, my good friend, and former dentist, Dr. William McColgen, cured me of the tropical fever. I was seeing the dentist on a regular basis for treatment of a tooth problem. The doctor gave me some strong medication for six weeks. This occurred around 1975, and I have not had one symptom of the disease since that time.

Dr. McColgen now lives in Louisiana. When I think of him, those thoughts usually end with thankfulness that he gave me back my life. I quoted this verse earlier, but it certainly applies here, as well: "Weeping may endure for a night, but joy cometh in the morning" (Psalm 30:5).

If a person reflected only on the frustration of life, then that person might develop the same attitude that was expressed by one biblical writer who said, "Vanity, vanity, all is vanity" (Psalm 39:5).

As I review scenes from my many years, I don't recall ever being literally thrown out of but one place. That was the hospital room of a Memphis legend. It was a most embarrassing episode on my list of negative experiences.

This performer had been a patient at Methodist-South Hospital in Memphis, Tennessee, for several weeks. I was aware that he was there but gave little further thought to his local presence. Methodist-South was an almost daily visit for me. The church where I was pastor at the time was located nearby, and many of the parishioners were patients at that hospital. The nurses knew me as one of the local pastors.

The room of this famed musician was located on the second floor, just across from the nurses' station. One afternoon, I had just passed the nurses' location when one of them approached me and said, "There is a very sick man in that room, and I'm sure he would be glad to see you."

Who the person was made little difference to me. A sick person is a sick person. If someone wanted to see me, I was always ready to talk with him. I was not told who the patient was.

The door was open; I spoke to him and was in the process of introducing myself. The patient raised his head from his pillow as his generous smile crossed his face. He appeared to be elated that even a stranger would visit him. I was also happy to be accepted in such a friendly fashion.

But that comfortable meeting was to be quickly terminated. Someone came from behind me and quickly placed an arm-lock on my right arm and began to back me toward the door. I was trying to explain my presence, but a hefty woman continued to apply pressure on my arm. By the time she backed me to the door, my anger had begun to rise. I highly resented being man-handled (or maybe I should say woman-handled).

It has been my experience in life that there are sometimes people around who can bring out the worst in others. I knew a thing or two about arm locks. I slung my arm away from my captor in such a fashion that it must have jarred her ancestors. At the same instant, I commanded her, "Get your hands off me, woman!"

She replied, "You can't come in here!"

My response was, "Woman, I was asked to come in here and see this patient. I don't even know who the person is."

She quickly said to me, "This is _____" (a renowned entertainer whose privacy I am respecting). Now comes the part that I have regretted for many years.

"This man's celebrity doesn't mean a thing," I replied.

My statement wasn't very truthful. After being greeted by such a pleasant smile and personal acceptance, I was very sorry that I said that in his presence. I have had a tender feeling for him every since that short meeting, but I have remembered his associate with a full measure of resentment and personal animosity. I hope I had cooled my temperament before I entered the room of the patient that I had come to see.

Many of my memories are pleasant. There stands a huge white-oak tree beside the field road that leads to our fish lake. That tree has withstood a strike by lightning, numerous storms, and at least one tornado. Today, it is healthy and continues to provide suitable shade for my cattle. There was once a hunter's cabin beside that tree, but it has been gone for many years. This very day, I passed by that place and, once again, pondered the times when my friends and I used the little house as our abode during our overnight camping.

Our camping events usually included between six and eight people. The expedition would last about two days and one night. We did a great deal of talking, a lot of eating, and some squirrel hunting.

One year, I had rented the farm to my neighboring farmer. The farmer had planted crops, in addition to a two-acre plot of fine late watermelons that were located near the woods where we were hunting. In the early fall, the night's dew fell on the crop, causing the fruit to be cool and tasty the next morning. That turned out to be an added attraction for our camping party. It was not only an attraction but also a temptation for people who loved various assortments of fruit.

The first person to leave the forest and make his way to the shade of the big oak was Charles McMahan, a neighbor from Ripley, Tennessee. Charles later told the rest of the party that as he came out, he very much wanted one of those melons. He then stated, "But the preacher is up here with us, and he might not appreciate my imposition on the farmer."

I was the second person to stop hunting that morning. I just happened to go by the melon patch and gather up two of those favorable fruits. From there to our camping area, the distance was about one-eighth of a mile. The sun had begun to express itself rather effectively, and my load almost exceeded my license for hauling.

I can still visualize Charles' expression as I wobbled my load into camp. When the rest of the hunters came from the woods, our friend revealed the rest of his story. "Here I was afraid to get one melon, and then I looked across the field, and here came the preacher carrying two!" Charles was most pleased to join the rest of us as we had our picnic around the outside table under the spreading limbs of Mother Nature.

The lifting of a watermelon from another person's field has been a much-discussed issue for as long as I can remember. Some people think it is all right to do so; others think it is sinful and amounts to theft. Each person is entitled to his or her own opinion. Personally, I think the matter is conditional.

This short story may help me to explain what I mean

by conditional. In 2002 and 2003, severe tornadoes hit Jackson, Tennessee, causing much damage and some loss of life. Those two storms missed our farm—ten miles outside of town—by only a short distance.

Shortly after the first tragedy, I had a prefabricated storm shelter installed near the back door of our house. I informed our neighbor, a man with four people in his family, that they were welcome to use the shelter if necessary. He asked, "How many will the storm shelter accommodate?"

I told him, "That depends on the intensity of the storm. If need be, we can sit on each other's laps."

The issue of plucking a neighbor's watermelon depends upon the circumstances at hand. I viewed our situation as a gift from a generous farmer. "He that is without sin, let him cast the first stone" (John 8:7). I don't want to be guilty of sermonizing at this point, but here you have my theory on the subject of nature verses humanity.

Those days present some fond memories for those of us who remain. As a person grows older, the so-called common things of life seem to become more and more valuable. Maybe, it is only then that a person is willing to pause long enough to "smell the roses."

All flowers do not grow on bushes or vines. Some come in the form of human beings. I have mentioned some already. I now add one more to the list.

I would be remiss if I did not mention this unique person. Pauline, my youngest sister, is a retired schoolteacher. Both she and her husband, Basil Snider, were involved in the various school systems in West Tennessee until their retirement many years ago.

Pauline has always had a ready ear for other people, often to the point of becoming stressful about their affairs.

218

I have said to her on some occasions, "You are just not mean enough to project your own individuality."

My sister's input in the experiences of my life has, for many years, been very significant. She was a source of motivation for me to finish college. She received her formal education some years after becoming employed by the Southern Bell Telephone Company. Pauline's advice to me was, "If I can do it, you can too."

After all these years, it remains vivid in my mind that she took time away from her employment and visited me while I was in basic training at Camp Gordon, Georgia. She may not have enjoyed that secluded weekend too well, but her presence was comforting to me. This was a kindness that left a lasting impression on me.

I believe the most stabilizing factor in a person's life is a sense of family. It is common knowledge that illness, circumstance, and fear can dilute the condition of loyalty, support, and appreciation for one's kin. These are some exceptions to the rule and not the general principle.

I will affirm that whatever may be wrong with me is not the fault of my family; however, what may be right with me, to a large degree, can be credited to my relatives. There have been occasions in my own life when these words from an old church hymnal spoke loudly and clearly: "I would be true for there are those who trust me."

My immediate family is small, but there is no shortage of love, encouragement, and appreciation for one another. In addition to myself, my family is composed of Christine, Jean, Ivan, Clay, and now, Clay's wife, Julie. Elizabeth, our granddaughter, is no longer with us. She left us at the age of thirteen. Yet, in our fond memories and in our hearts, she will always be present. I will not comment any further on individual members. As a whole, we enjoy a common bond of personal love and unity.

I am aware that I have stripped the family tree quite bare. I began by relating some information about where I came from. Now, I have revealed my whereabouts. I am happy in my current location. In fact, I am happy just to still be located!

When writing this manuscript, I often used the word "I," but I had a large number of people in mind at all times. That includes the person now reading this book. If I were to have the pleasure of hearing your life story, I would be most honored.

If I happened to find myself in a patient mood, I might even be willing to hear Robert Sikes' rendition, again. Thanks, Mr. Sikes, or whoever you were. The note that you never honored is considered "paid in full."

Epilogue

Why Do Good Men Go Bad?

I do not really know the answer to the question, "Why do good men become bad?" I have raised more questions in this writing than I have answered. It is my basic assumption that if a person becomes bad, then he or she was never really good to begin with. That individual was like a wreck about to happen. All he needed was an excuse, prodding, or permission to carry out the acts of a dirty, selfish, resentful mind and spirit.

As I sought to deal with factors like love, compassion, trust, patience, etc., I was aware that military training and discipline has turned thousands of kind folks into killers for the purpose of national security. Many war veterans were able to readjust to peaceful modes of life, while others were never able or willing to make a positive adjustment for peace. I think this comes under the heading of forced negative conditioning.

But the question I have in mind is, "Why do people who have a normal opportunity for peaceful living turn to violence and immorality?" I have sought to use reason, theology, public opinion, history, the horrors of war, social science, and the impact of sin and virtue to understand the conflict between good and evil. It is immaterial to me that Robert Sikes was able to con me out of $150. My concern is why people do as they do. What motivated this highly skilled person to succumb to a trade that was beneath his intellect, ability, and dignity? I do not imagine that the 30 pieces of silver Judas got for betraying Jesus did him much good, and in this day and time, I do not imagine those few dollars did my betrayer much good either. Reason cannot remove the dichotomy in man that is caused by the battle between good and evil.

These two examples reveal degrees of evil, but both are symptoms of negative socialization, to say the least. I thoroughly disagree with former President of the United States, Richard M. Nixon, who, when speaking to his White House Staff immediately prior to his resignation from the presidency, said, "The judgment of history depends upon who writes it." I think it is more appropriate to say that history depends upon the contributions of each participant who leaves his or her mark upon human experience in order to make it worthy of duplication.

In this case, the facts speak for themselves. Robert Sikes was an unsocialized being living in a world that was created to be civilized. From my point of view, this was a most unusual example of insecurity growing into an infectious morality and causing mental destruction.

Life is like a swinging door. It opens either way, and one may carry through it what he or she wishes. It is up to each person to decide whether his luggage will be good or evil.

In this writing, I have told some long stories; I think it is plain to see that each individual chooses his destiny.

As I reflect on what I have written, I have not sought to tell a portion of my life's story, but to reflect upon our story—the story of humanity. I am 79 years of age. Like

John Walker of Blytheville, Arkansas, I have had a good life, although it has not been as fault-free or productive as it should have been. Sometimes I humorously but truthfully say that my wife, Christine, and our lovely daughter, Jean, always wanted to make me more than I wanted to be. But now I am more prone to count my blessings than to recall my adversities.

Personal appreciation is hereby extended to my family; my friends in all of the churches I have served; my good and loyal comrades in the military service (some of whom aided my longevity of life); all of my teachers and instructors in school; but most of all, to God, who has opened to me the doors of countless opportunities—some of which I have entered with fear and trembling, but I trust, always with much gratitude and humility.

If I could live my life again, there are many things I would skip and many I would do differently, but I am aware that we pass this way but once. Each of us needs to enter the best avenues of life and keep on moving. The travel may be hard at times, but the rewards will be unlimited.

Recently, a friend of mine, a mortician, said to me, "Every time we bury a person, we bury a book." Personally, I still have many fish yet to fry, so I prefer to wait a while for the first and offer this "traveler's log" in the meantime. I can only hope that *Voyage of a Veteran* and the thoughts of its now 80-year-old sojourner will resonate with each of you. May God's blessing be on you all.

Endnotes

1 Virginia R. Mollenkott, *In Search of Balance* (Waco, Texas: Word Books, Publisher, 1969), p. 13.

2 Roger L. Shinn, *Wars and Rumors of Wars* (Nashville and New York: Abingdon Press, 1972), pp. 272-273.

3 Martin E. Marty, *By Way of Response* (Nashville and New York: Abingdon Press, 1981), p. 20.

4 *The Upper Room Disciplines for 1977*, p. 174.

5 *The Cumberland Seminarian*, Volume XXI, 1983, p. 5.

6 Mollenkott, *op. cit*, p. 14.

7 Marty, *op. cit.*

8 Henry T. Sell, *Prayer Meeting Talks* (Grand Rapids, Michigan: Baker Book House, 1972), p. 101.

9 Henry T. Sell, *op cit.*, p. 108.

10 James D. Smart, *Doorway To A New Age* (Board of Missions, United Methodist Church, 475 Riverside Drive, New York, N.Y.), p. 67.

11 Chester A. Pennington, *Even So Believe* (Nashville, New York: Abingdon Press, 1966), p. 44.

12 G. Byron Deshler, *Finding The Truth About God* (Nashville, Tennessee, 1964), p. 57.

13 Carol Matteson Cox, *Jubilee Time*, (Nashville: Abingdon Press, 1984), p. 11 (As quoted by Bishop Roy Colvin Nichols)

14 Thomas Lane Butts, *Tigers in the Dark* (Nashville: Abingdon Press, 1978), p. 101.

15 *Ibid*, p. 42.

16 John T. Seaman, *On Tiptoe With Joy* (Kansas City, Missouri: Beacon Hill Press, 1967), p. 83.

17 Helmut Thielicke, *Out of the Depths* (Grand Rapids, Michigan, William B. Eerdmans Publishing Company, 1962), p. 11.

18 William Barclay, *Daily Celebration* (Waco Texas: Word Books, Publisher, 1976), p. 91.

19 Ralph W. Sockman, *The Paradoxes of Jesus* (New York, Cincinnati, Chicago: The Abingdon Press, 1928), p. 16.

20 Lillian Eichler Watson, *Lights From Many Lamps* (New York: Simon and Schuster, 1951), p. 83.

About the Author

Russell Lowell Reid is a veteran of World War II and a retired minister of the United Methodist Church. Reid grew up with seven siblings on the family farm in rural Madison County and served in the United States Army from 1945-1946. His full-time Christian ministry began in 1961. A graduate of then Lambuth College and Memphis Theological Seminary, he is married to the former Christine Drake. The two will soon mark 60 years of marriage. They have one daughter Jean and now reside in Ripley, Tennessee.

Printed in the United States
61496LVS00002B/61-147